PRAISE FOR *THE JOU*

"In *The Journey Home* Meredith reaches the hearts of her read... disarmingly gentle yet powerful depths. While affirming the grace of Christ, she also welcomes us toward our essential callings, beckoning us to courageous spiritual practices that will lead us to the truest freedoms this world can offer—even as we wait for the next."

—CHRISTA HARDIN, HOST OF *ENNEAGRAM + MARRIAGE* PODCAST

"Meredith shows up passionately as our coach on page one, fully committed to seeing us reach our full God-given potential, with words that are punchy yet vulnerable and profound yet crystal clear."

—TYLER ZACH, AUTHOR OF THE GOSPEL FOR
ENNEAGRAM DEVOTIONAL SERIES

"*The Journey Home* is so needed in the ongoing Enneagram conversation. Meredith does a fantastic job framing the Enneagram in a biblical worldview, tackling hard questions about its origin, and sharing practical ways to apply its wisdom to our lives."

—RACHEL CRUZE, #1 *NEW YORK TIMES* BESTSELLING
AUTHOR AND HOST OF *THE RACHEL CRUZE SHOW*

"Whether you're an Enneagram expert or you've never heard of the Enneagram, *The Journey Home* is for you. Meredith does a great job educating, challenging, and empowering readers through her candor and expertise, while also keeping our eyes on what matters most, our faith."

—MANDY JOHNSON, WRITER FEATURED IN PROVERBS
31 MINISTRIES, DAUGHTER OF DELIGHT, AND
FELLOWSHIP OF CHRISTIAN ATHLETES

"Meredith has done a beautiful job in presenting the Enneagram as a positive tool for believers while keeping our focus on the gospel. She gives us practical advice to strengthen our relationship with God and others while challenging us to dig deep and put in the work ourselves. *The Journey Home* will leave you convicted to never lose sight of Jesus in a world where everyone wants to 'self-reflect.'"

—NICOLE JACOBSMEYER, AUTHOR OF *TAKE BACK YOUR JOY*

"The Enneagram has long been an insightful and simultaneously a deeply convicting tool for me—both as a therapist and as a believer. In working with the Enneagram, we need guides who can lead us with direct, illuminating truth and expansive amounts of grace. I'm grateful Meredith is now bringing that truth and grace to all of us through the pages of this book."

—SISSY GOFF, MED, LPC-MHSP, CCATP, DIRECTOR OF
CHILD AND ADOLESCENT COUNSELING AT DAYSTAR
COUNSELING, HOST OF THE *RAISING BOYS AND GIRLS*
PODCAST, AND AUTHOR OF *RAISING WORRY-FREE GIRLS*

"*The Journey Home* meets an essential need—bringing awareness to our need for God's love and truth and finding safety in His care for us no matter what our individual weaknesses/strengths may be. This book gave me permission to explore difficult sides of myself without judgment and discover the gift of how God uniquely made me to care for myself and others."

—BAILEY T. HURLEY, AUTHOR OF *TOGETHER IS A BEAUTIFUL PLACE*

"Of all there is to recommend about this book, what I love most is that in these chapters the topic of the Enneagram is submitted to a conservative and high view of Scripture. Drawing from conversations with many people, Meredith creates a narrative put forth in a thoughtful storytelling style. More than just the truth of this text, I love her heart to help lead people either into or back into a vibrant faith."

—TONY WOOD, DOVE AWARD-WINNING SONGWRITER
AND AUTHOR OF *A PARENTS BOOK OF PRAYERS*

"Drawing off her own journey to know her deeper and truer self, Meredith guides readers on a wonderful adventure to not merely understand the Enneagram, but to travel a sacred pathway that will help them discover a deeper sense of self, identity, and purpose in life. *The Journey Home* is an easy-to-read field manual that will help you navigate the terrain of your heart as you integrate your life story, the Enneagram, and the gospel. So get comfortable and enjoy the journey—the journey home."

—JEFF AND LORA HELTON, AUTHORS OF THE
50 FRIDAYS MARRIAGE CHALLENGE

"My generation has often responded to the Enneagram in one of two extremes: we discount it or we define ourselves by it. In *The Journey Home* Meredith gently untangles many misconceptions and addresses the subtle but dangerous nuances of both sides. Her words are compelling. Wise. Practical. I couldn't stop reading! Each chapter is equally gripping and created a safe space for me to travel that murky, sometimes scary path inward to encounter both God and myself in a fresh, truer, and transformative way."

—TAYLOR JOY MURRAY, AUTHOR OF *STOP SAYING I'M FINE*

"With humility and grace Meredith invites us into her own journey back home to God, showing us practically how to begin the journey as well. Her voice is so needed in this self-help crazed world, because while the Enneagram is an excellent tool, she never stops reminding us through the pages of *The Journey Home* to keep our eyes fixed on Jesus, where true transformation happens."

—JULIE BUSLER, AUTHOR OF *JOYFUL SORROW*

"This is the most impactful book on the Enneagram that I've read. As I made tough but good decisions, I noticed an immediate shift into what felt like a journey home towards myself. This book has impacted my spiritual life and walk with God in a monumental way."

—KELSEY CHAPMAN, AUTHOR OF *WHAT THEY TAUGHT ME*

"This is the Enneagram resource I've been looking for for years! In her masterful work, *The Journey Home*, Meredith offers a refreshing and healthy approach to the Enneagram—one that doesn't eclipse the gospel, but rather yields to the gospel as we understand our God-given uniqueness and pursue relational wholeness. Take your time with this important book. There is a wealth of wisdom on these pages!"

—NICOLE ZASOWSKI, MARRIAGE AND FAMILY THERAPIST AND AUTHOR OF *WHAT IF IT'S WONDERFUL?*

"Each page of *The Journey Home* gave me the gift of self-awareness and (even better) the gift of Christ-awareness. As a bold and honest Eight, Meredith challenges us to aggressively cooperate with God along our journey of spiritual transformation. Even better, she gives us practical tools to make that transformation a daily reality."

—RACHEL SIMS MILLER, SPEECHWRITER AT
RAMSEY SOLUTIONS AND AUTHOR

"It's so easy to let anything but the gospel truth become your gospel truth—Enneagram included. With great knowledge and wisdom, Meredith continuously brings us back to our one true savior and invites us into a reenergized faith using the Enneagram as a catalyst. She beautifully brings the two worlds together while keeping the main thing the main thing."

—JOHANNA VANN, COPYWRITER AND AUTHOR

"Meredith encourages us to think, guiding us to reach our own conclusions by leading us to her well of written words and letting us choose what works for us. For an Enneagram novice, *The Journey Home* was an eye-opening experience."

—CAROLE HOLIDAY, AUTHOR

"As a therapist, I've spent years reading about the Enneagram, but I never felt that I really grasped how to apply it in my day-to-day life or in my practice. Learning about the Enneagram always felt daunting and overwhelming. *The Journey Home* answers this need in a big way. Each chapter teaches how we can grow both emotionally and spiritually while using this incredible tool. *The Journey Home* finally makes the Enneagram user friendly and incredibly applicable to followers of Jesus."

—RACHAEL ELMORE, MA, LCMHC-S, NCC, AUTHOR

"This is the Enneagram book for those who want to mature in their faith without getting Enneagram-obsessed. It's honest, enlightening, approachable, and written by an Eight—which means it's truth wrapped up in a warm hug and, other times, a punch to your gut. Basically, it's the best."

—HANNA SEYMOUR, AUTHOR OF *THE COLLEGE GIRL'S SURVIVAL GUIDE*, HOST OF *NO MATTER WHAT* PODCAST, AND BIBLE TEACHER

THE
JOURNEY
HOME

A Biblical Guide TO Using the Enneagram TO Deepen Your Faith AND Relationships

MEREDITH BOGGS

NELSON
BOOKS

An Imprint of Thomas Nelson

The Journey Home

© 2023 by Meredith Boggs

Published in Nashville, Tennessee, by Nelson Books, an imprint of Thomas Nelson. Nelson Books and Thomas Nelson are registered trademarks of HarperCollins Christian Publishing, Inc.

Published in association with COMPEL, a writers community founded by Lysa TerKeurst.

Published in association with the literary agency of Brock, Inc., P.O. Box 384, Matthews, NC 28105.

Thomas Nelson titles may be purchased in bulk for educational, business, fundraising, or sales promotional use. For information, please email SpecialMarkets@ThomasNelson.com.

Unless otherwise noted, Scripture quotations are taken from the ESV® Bible (The Holy Bible, English Standard Version®). Copyright © 2001 by Crossway, a publishing ministry of Good News Publishers. Used by permission. All rights reserved.

Scripture quotations marked NASB and NASB1995 are taken from the New American Standard Bible® (NASB). Copyright © 1960, 1962, 1963, 1968, 1971, 1972, 1973, 1975, 1977, 1995 by The Lockman Foundation. Used by permission. www.lockman.org

Scripture quotations marked NIV are taken from The Holy Bible, New International Version®, NIV®. Copyright © 1973, 1978, 1984, 2011 by Biblica, Inc.® Used by permission of Zondervan. All rights reserved worldwide. www.Zondervan.com. The "NIV" and "New International Version" are trademarks registered in the United States Patent and Trademark Office by Biblica, Inc.®

The graph on page 150 was used by permission from Chip Dodd.

Most names have been changed and stories summarized to honor and protect individual identities.

Library of Congress Cataloging-in-Publication Data

Names: Boggs, Meredith, 1990- author.
Title: The Journey home : a Biblical guide to using the enneagram to deepen your faith and relationships / Meredith Boggs.
Description: Nashville, Tennessee : Thomas Nelson, 2022. | Summary: "Certified Enneagram teacher Meredith Boggs gives Christians who are skeptical of the Enneagram a conservative biblical guide to understand how it can further their spiritual journeys and deepen their relationship with God by discovering their type's virtues, unhelpful tendencies, and best practices for spiritual growth"-- Provided by publisher.
Identifiers: LCCN 2022028210 (print) | LCCN 2022028211 (ebook) | ISBN 9781400233939 (h/c) | ISBN 9781400233977 (ebook)
Subjects: LCSH: Spirituality--Christianity. | Spiritual life--Christianity. | Enneagram.
Classification: LCC BV4501.3 .B6455 2022 (print) | LCC BV4501.3 (ebook) | DDC 248.4--dc23/eng/20220826
LC record available at https://lccn.loc.gov/2022028210
LC ebook record available at https://lccn.loc.gov/2022028211ISBN 978-1-4002-3393-9

Printed in the United States of America

23 24 25 26 27   LSC   10 9 8 7 6 5 4 3 2 1

Dad, to borrow your own words: your love gave me roots and helped me find my wings. I always wanted to be a writer just like you. Now it just feels official.

CONTENTS

CONTENTS

FOREWORD

I REMEMBER HEARING A PODCAST EPISODE about the Enneagram by Meredith and her husband, Justin, back in 2019. Their practical knowledge about the Enneagram made their podcast one of my go-to recommendations for my coaching clients. The ability to teach something so complex with such clarity and biblical insight is a true gift. I am so glad Meredith has continued to use her gifting to teach about the Enneagram and how it can be a phenomenal tool for growth.

I have been a lifelong searcher of purpose and identity, asking myself questions like, *Who am I? Why am I here? What should I do next?* This drive has drawn me to personal discovery tools, from Myers-Briggs Type Indicator tests to random Buzzfeed quizzes about what kind of food I would be. I wanted to know who I was. I wanted to have a name for what being me was like.

In 2017 I received my first Enneagram book, which started a new journey of self-discovery for me. My life has shifted in big ways for the better since Enneagram became my second language, but the journey happened in steps, not in one easy swoop.

First came shame. The discovery of my Enneagram type initially felt like a slap to the face. Everything I had tried so hard not to be was suddenly named as my own. Being told who I was with such clarity made me feel nauseous—and so vulnerable. This is a part of the journey of self-awareness, and one that I think confirms your typing better than almost anything else.

Second, the accuracy of my type grabbed hold in a near obsessive way. After reeling from the pain of discovering I was a Four, all I wanted was to learn more. Understand more. Put myself under this microscope. I did this not to excuse all that I was, but to learn how to become someone who looked more like Christ. Self-awareness shows you where to look for the problems in your life. Your relationship with Christ will guide you in the growing part.

Finally, or rather currently, I've loved sharing with others how using this tool is a means to growing in Christ and having more grace for others. I don't believe the Enneagram is vital to everyone's spiritual growth, but for those who use it in tandem with their knowledge of God, it can be very powerful—near life changing.

No matter where you are in your own Enneagram journey, I want to give you one piece of advice: Keep going with eyes fixed on your Savior. Don't hide from the yuck of self; use your knowledge to kill sin and let God grow what he called good in creating you. If the Enneagram teaches us anything, it's that our best and worst parts are often just different sides of the same coin.

When God calls you a new creation, he is not asking you to stop being a person with a personality. He is shifting the focus of your life from yourself to him. Your personality, skills, talents, and quirks can bring him glory when your life is focused on him.

I love how Meredith has highlighted the messiness of our personalities, the Enneagram as a tool, and how all of that is nothing without Christ redeeming our story. *The Journey Home* is more than a mere collection of information—it's a hand to help guide you through the muck and mire of initial self-awareness to the holy ground of healing and growing in Christlikeness. As you begin these pages, let those initial feelings of exposure—which tempt you to look away—remind you instead to lean in. You are in the thick of growing, friend.

—Elisabeth Bennett, certified Enneagram life coach

INTRODUCTION

For My Threes, Sevens, and Eights

AS A TYPE EIGHT, I NEVER READ INTRODUCTIONS.
I just get right to it.

So here's the bottom line:

- The Enneagram is not the gospel.
- The Enneagram can help you grow personally and spiritually, but don't use it to replace God's Word. That will lead you astray more than any cult.
- You are not your type.
- The quickest way to get stalled out, stuck, and hopelessly lost is to label yourself, confine yourself to your type, and use it as an excuse for bad behavior. Also, don't do that to other people—it's damaging.
- If you don't like or agree with this book, that's fine. I wrote it anyway.

"Don't be too self-aware or you'll lose sight of Jesus." Those words spoken by a wise woman, Diane Reason, whom I was lucky enough to gain as a grandmother by marriage, are ones that have guided me on my personal Enneagram journey.

Yes, grow in self-awareness, always. Keep leaning in, keep learning, keep growing, keep asking questions and peeling back layers to discover what's underneath. But self-awareness isn't the endgame. It's Jesus. Only Jesus.

For Everyone Else

Whether you can name a specific situation or conversation that triggered the beginning of your spiritual drift, it's there. For many of you, growing up in the church and making a profession of faith at a young age was the norm. But if we jump several years to high school, college, and into young adulthood, that fiery passion for Christ, which burned within your bones during that post-camp high or after coming home from your first international mission trip, has dwindled. The mere ember of a flame that once flickered in your soul has all but been snuffed out by the stagnant and stuck feeling that weighs on you. Disenchanted with your faith and thoroughly disinterested, you wish you cared more—you *want* to care more—but you just don't.

To add to the mess and confusion, maybe your last church really burned you bad. So bad you considered throwing in the towel. With lingering hurt left from the church you once called home and the well-meaning fellow believers who tried to force you into a Christian mold you were never created to fit into, you're over it. While you didn't officially give up on all things church related, you would hardly consider yourself an active member of the church you attend. That is, the one you attend when you haven't been out too late the night before or aren't too exhausted from the workweek to peel yourself out of bed and slip into the back row wearing your Sunday best. And since the pandemic forced you into a new rhythm of life, you may never have a reason to step foot through the sanctuary doors again, now that curling up on your couch with coffee for virtual church is the new Sunday-morning norm.

You never anticipated being here spiritually, but who does?

Now you're wondering how to get back to a place of spiritual wellness. With its reemergence in recent years, maybe the Enneagram has piqued your interest. You may have googled all the free tests out there or heard enough about the concept to solidify your type. Perhaps you found a deep resonance with your type, like being known in a way you never have before and given a language you previously didn't have the skills to speak.

The Enneagram has provided a framework to understand how you interact with the world and how you relate to your type Six colleague, your type One mom, and your type Three best friend. You've laughed hard at the scary accuracy of the memes about your Enneagram type that you see as you scroll through Instagram. You've come to new levels of awareness about yourself, even parts of you that date back to childhood experiences. Maybe you've even cried at the parts of yourself you've discovered or recovered, which you thought were a distant memory at best. This self-discovery has brought hope for who you are capable of becoming on this personal-growth trajectory.

But the unexpected part of this Enneagram journey is that it has simultaneously intensified the pain of disconnection from God and caused the loneliness and estrangement from Christian community to persist. You thought you were over it—and you are over the well-meaning but fake feeling of community. Yet you realize you're not completely over it; you feel a deep sadness and aching loneliness for the spiritual community and connection that has vanished.

The Enneagram is not the gospel, nor am I promoting the Enneagram over the gospel in any way. The gospel will forever stand alone in its certainty and authority. The Enneagram is merely a tool that, when utilized well, can help guide you back to God. It has the potential to illuminate how you were uniquely created, perfectly designed by God, originally in your truest essence. It provides a construct, showing us how we all can become lost in this world, wandering from the heart of God in our sinful tendencies and godless fixations. It highlights the lies that keep us in bondage and the truths that are a healing balm to our souls. But it can never be a substitute or replace the authoritative Word of God in our spiritual journey.

If you're a weary traveler or a spiritual vagabond or find yourself holding on to threadbare hope that *maybe* the connection and community you once knew is still possible, I believe you have this book in your hands for a reason. Throughout this book, we will journey together through the Enneagram types, triads, and sin proclivities that separate us from God and others. We'll look at each type's virtue and essence, which are a testament to astonishing goodness and beauty. My prayer is that, with a pathway toward transformation, you will discover the reconnection with God your soul so desperately longs for as you journey home to yourself and him.

PART ONE

Charting the Course

1

ORIGINS OF THE
ENNEAGRAM

THE ORIGIN OF THE ENNEAGRAM AND debate on whether Christians should be utilizing it and engaging with it, given its nonbiblical history, have surfaced in evangelical spaces. With the Enneagram's increasing prominence in recent years, discussions began about it being rooted in mysticism and derived from the occult world, and it would be unwise to ignore these claims and not dig into its history. While it's tough to say where the Enneagram originated, I'm not compelled to try to convince you that it was rooted in Christianity or to defend its origins. There's not a lot of clear evidence about its origins, since it began as an oral tradition. The roots of the Enneagram can be traced back to fourth-century Desert Fathers and Evagrius Ponticus, a Greek Christian contemplative whose works contained Enneagram-like symbols and the "eight evil thoughts," which later become known more famously as the "seven deadly sins." The ancient wisdom of the Enneagram was derived from a time period in the Middle East when there was comingling of many religious influences including Christian, Hellenistic, Sufi, Buddhist, and Hindu traditions.[1]

The Enneagram as we know it today with its nine personality types was formally systemized by Oscar Ichazo, a Bolivian-born philosopher. George Gurdjieff is attributed with reintroducing the Enneagram symbol to the modern world; however, his work did not incorporate personality types. He was the founder of a school for inner work, and his teachings in general are deeply interwoven with cosmology and the metaphysical. The Enneagram came to spiritual leaders in the US by way of Claudio Naranjo, a Chilean-born psychiatrist who studied with Ichazo and was considered a pioneer in integrating psychotherapy with spiritual traditions.[2] Franciscan priest Richard Rohr, author Helen Palmer, and founders of the Enneagram Institute, Don Richard Riso and Russ Hudson, are notable influences of the Enneagram as we know it today. The tradition has been brought even further into the Christian sphere by people such as Ian Morgan Cron and Suzanne Stabile.

Most early teachers did not subscribe to a biblical worldview. This is why Tyler Zach—a friend, pastor, and fellow Enneagram teacher—as well as others, such as Beth and Jeff McCord of Your Enneagram Coach and author Elisabeth Bennett, have made it their mission to approach the Enneagram with a biblical worldview as they lead and teach others.

Where the concern has been raised is with the esoteric teachers, namely Gurdjieff, but also Ichazo and Naranjo, who have strongly influenced the Enneagram as we know it. If you want to go down a deep rabbit hole (for all my type Fives reading along), check out Marcia Montenegro and Don and Joy Veinot, who are boisterous opponents of the Enneagram based on some of what we know about these teachers.

Some will argue that the Enneagram is fully rooted within the Christian tradition, but it isn't. It's a spiritual hodgepodge derived from differing religions, philosophers, and teachers. Regardless, it can be part of the spiritual framework of your Christian journey. Many professing believers have found other personality-assessment tools helpful in understanding themselves—for example, the MBTI (Myers-Briggs Type Indicator), DiSC (Dominance, Influence, Steadiness, and Conscientiousness), and StrengthsFinder. While any of these tools can be an asset in forging your personal growth and subsequently your spiritual path, they have resonated strongly with younger evangelicals and millennials who may have wandered from the formal institution of the church but are still in search of ways to augment their faith. These groups in particular are seeking additional tools, like the Enneagram, when they desire a deeply connected relationship with God yet aren't sure how to find their way.

The Enneagram has the ability to bring about a greater awareness of self, which, if stewarded well and held in the proper posture, can lead us back to the heart of God. John Calvin spoke to the importance and interconnectedness of self-knowledge and knowledge of God in *The Institutes of the Christian Religion*: "The knowledge of God and that of ourselves are connected. Without knowledge of self, there is no knowledge of God. Without knowledge of God there is no knowledge of self."[3] The Enneagram can bring about tremendous self-knowledge and awareness, which is why I believe there has been such a deep resonance with it.

So what do we do with the uncertain origin of the Enneagram?

Is it unwise to use it?

Do we write it off entirely?

Do we use it carefully and cautiously?

When approaching the Enneagram as a Christian, it's important to look at it through the lens of a biblical worldview, which we should be doing each day as we engage the culture around us. We read online articles, listen to podcasts, watch news clips, and have conversations with friends and colleagues, and it's our responsibility to filter these through a biblical worldview. I'd venture to say there's *value* in exposure to ideas and beliefs that *do not* fit into our paradigm and instead stretch us to think beyond our own bubble. Beyond that, I believe there is wisdom in exploring ideas and beliefs not explicitly tied to Scripture.

A compelling consideration about utilizing the Enneagram as a Christian comes from the doctrines of *general revelation* and *special revelation*. Special revelation is how God has made himself known to mankind through the written scriptures, the Bible. Hebrews 1:1–3a tells us, "Long ago, at many times and in many ways, God spoke to our fathers by the prophets, but in these last days he has spoken to us by his Son, whom he appointed the heir of all things, through whom also he created the world. He is the radiance of the glory of God and the exact imprint of his nature, and he upholds the universe by the word of his power." God revealed and continues to reveal himself to us through the written gospel accounts and through the ancient texts of the Bible.

Pastor and author James Abrahamson, who was trained at Dallas Theological Seminary, wrote, "Special revelation is that self-disclosure of God and unveiling of truths that expand and transcend the General Revelation of creation, culture, and conscience."[4] Conversely, there is general revelation of God amid creation that is intuitive. Psalm 19:1–3 speaks to this intuitive sense: "The heavens are telling of the glory of God; and their expanse is declaring the work of His hands. Day to day pours forth speech, and night to night reveals knowledge. There is no speech, nor are there words; their voice is not heard" (NASB1995). We look at the expanse of the skies, the stars arrayed in all their shimmering glory, and we just *know* in our soul that there is something bigger than us, that there *has* to be a God. That is what general revelation speaks to.

God has been revealing himself to us since the beginning of creation. In his kindness, he continues to reveal himself to us in many ways: through creation, through Scripture spanning different centuries and cultures, and even through the all-encompassing common grace.

In his book *Every Good Endeavor*, Timothy Keller wrote,

> Without an understanding of common grace, Christians will believe they can live self-sufficiently within their own cultural enclave . . . Mozart was a gift to us—whether he was a believer or not. So Christians are free to study the world of human culture in order to know more of God; for as creatures made in His image we can appreciate truth and wisdom wherever we find it.[5]

The secular culture around us can teach us truth; it can tell us something about God. We can gain wisdom from secular ideas and influences without adopting them and assimilating into them.

Because all mankind was created in the image of God, something about us makes the goodness, beauty, and truth of God known to the rest of the world; his essence is imprinted on us. We are his image bearers. Thus, what we create, the work of our hands, reflects his essence and image. Whether we create music or art, raise babies, build businesses, or play integral roles in large corporations, traces of God's goodness, beauty, and truth will always be in our work.

If we limit ourselves to consuming strictly "Christian" content only, shopping at Christian-led businesses, and creating a closely knit circle of Christian influences, we are not able to engage with the culture around us in a way that will make a meaningful and lasting impact in the course of redemptive history. While we must be careful how we filter the content we consume and the influences we subject ourselves to, we shouldn't avoid them altogether, because if we were to do so, we would miss out on the wisdom we may otherwise glean, the understanding we may otherwise come to, and the compassion we otherwise would have for humankind.

You can disagree with someone's cultural, biblical, and spiritual worldview while still finding value in their content, still learning something about yourself, others, or God. You don't have to apply their principles and practices to your own life. There's wisdom to be gained and ways to grow from exposure to ideas and beliefs that do not fit in your faith paradigm. If your belief system is never tested or challenged, if you never exercise your mind by confronting a worldview that could counter or complement your own, how will you grow in wisdom and knowledge and truth?

If the origins of the Enneagram sound a little questionable, like you might be opening the door to the devil and it leaves you leery, you're not alone. I've had to explore the idea that meaningful perspectives outside of my own spiritual framework could potentially offer wisdom and insight. While it may seem like a silly comparison, I was in elementary and middle school when the Harry Potter books became wildly popular. It was hotly debated within the southern Bible Belt community I grew up in whether children in Christian families should be allowed to read them because the story was about a wizard and his comrades attending a school of witchcraft and wizardry.

Because my parents had to heavily incentivize (bribe) me to read anything more than the back of the cereal box, I genuinely found it shocking (and stupid) that anyone would want to read books of that length anyway. Nonetheless, the Harry Potter books were all the rage, and I had several friends banned from reading them simply because their parents feared their children would shift from nice, polite ten-year-olds to devil-worshiping Wiccans.

As a parent myself now, I understand a bit more where those parents were coming from. And I empathize, because it's important to seek wisdom and discernment as you make decisions for your precious children, genuinely desiring their best interests. While being interviewed, J. K. Rowling, author of the Harry Potter books, once said, "I have yet to meet a single child who's told me that they want to be a satanist or is particularly interested in the occult because of the book."[6] And I would say the same about the Enneagram. In my fifteen-plus years of learning, teaching, and writing about the Enneagram, I have yet to encounter one person who has converted to New Ageism, who started engaging in occult practices, or who walked away from the Christian faith for the mystical, metaphysical spiritual realm due to the Enneagram.

However, if the history of the Enneagram—or the Enneagram itself—is a stumbling block for you, do not read this book. If you are conflicted and hesitant because of its origin and it just doesn't sit right with you, throw this book in the garbage and never speak of it again. I'm serious. Because the Enneagram is not the gospel. The Word of God, the Bible, "is living and active, sharper than any two-edged sword, piercing to the division of soul and of spirit, of joints and of marrow, and discerning the thoughts and intentions of the heart," as Hebrews 4:12–13 states. The Bible will forever stand in its supreme authority and inerrancy, so I implore you to never set down your Bible to pick up a book about the Enneagram or any other book that one day moth and rust will destroy. Utilize the Enneagram as a tool to understand and grow but never as a substitute for the Word of God. That is treacherous territory.

This chapter has caused me to wrestle, praying for wisdom and discernment with each word that I type. I do not take lightly the task that is set before me, stewarding my words and the fact that you have picked up this book to support you in your spiritual journey of coming back home to God. I've spent long hours in thought and prayer over this book. It's entirely possible that five or ten years from now, I will say, do, learn, or come to believe something that will contradict, negate, nullify, repeal, or differ from what is in this book. And with cancel culture at a fevered pitch at this very moment, that makes it even more scary to write this. I am a human, just like you, just like every other person who has been canceled for whatever reason. If this book is what gets me culturally canceled at some point, so be it, because I hope that I continue to grow, learn, and change. I pray that the journey of sanctification and spiritual growth I am on will propel me to a very different place than where I am today.

Whether you are an invigorated evangelical or a skeptic who is now disenchanted by your former zeal, my prayer is that this book will help propel you along your spiritual journey. And at the same time, as much as I am committed to writing and speaking and I'm continually in prayer as I steward those gifts, I urge you to pick up your Bible. Dive into the Word of God and find out what it says about sin and sanctification, spiritual gifts, and the fruit of the Spirit. Your very life depends on it, and this book in no way can ever substitute for the Bible. In Philippians 2:12–13 Paul wrote,

> Therefore, my beloved, as you have always obeyed, so now, not only as in my presence but much more in my absence, work out your own salvation with fear and trembling, for it is God who works in you, both to will and to work for his good pleasure.

So the work is yours to do. Whether you move forward using this framework as a supportive tool in your walk with God or you put it down due to a conviction that this is not the right fit for your spiritual journey is between you and God. Don't just take my word for it—or blindly accept what the pastor said from the pulpit or on the podcast.

In an article for The Gospel Coalition, author and pastor Joe Carter sums up well the issue of the Enneagram's origins and how it has trickled into the evangelical world:

Evangelicals concerned about the Enneagram should probably worry less, since it's likely a mostly harmless fad that will fade away in a few years. And evangelicals enthralled with the Enneagram should probably wonder why they're spending so much energy on a tool that has about as much scientific validity as the four humors theory of Hippocrates.[7]

For you bottom-liners, if the Enneagram helps you, great. If it causes you to stumble, throw it out. As 1 Corinthians 10:23 says, "All things are permitted, but not all things are of benefit. All things are permitted, but not all things build people up" (NASB). The Bible alone has authority and power.

2

THE JOURNEY HOME

AS A MILLENNIAL WHO GREW UP IN THE
church, I must have prayed "the sinner's prayer" a million times
to make sure it "took." I sincerely loved Jesus and wanted to follow him and his plans for my life. For those who didn't have an
alter call every Sunday to publicly profess your newfound faith,
the sinner's prayer is a scripted proclamation of repentance for
your sin, acceptance of forgiveness, and profession of Jesus Christ
as your Lord and Savior.

Fast forward through a high school eating disorder, a relapse
in college, and the split of the church I grew up in, until I reached
young adulthood, where I found myself married to my high
school sweetheart, Justin. I had recently turned twenty-five years
old, and we were living abroad while working for a nonprofit
organization in China that provided medical and surgical care
for orphaned children. It had been an extremely rewarding but
intensely difficult year. Working long days with sick kiddos, we
watched them grow, hit milestones, and survive surgeries from

life-threatening heart defects. We were also confronted with the task of making decisions no one should ever have to make about when to continue escalating care or when to shift to comfort care, rocking those little ones as they crossed the thin veil from earth into eternity. But during that year I experienced some of the most personal, intimate, and connected moments I've ever had with God, having it out with him about how I really felt about his providence and sovereignty, hashing out his supposed goodness amid such tragedy and trauma.

Establishing Christian community during that time was a challenge. Our days were filled with hospital rounds from the time we woke up until evening hours. The city we lived in was rural, and with limited time and energy to venture out, our interaction with others was confined to the people working for the organization and house church once a week with those same fifteen people. Some of them rubbed me the wrong way or annoyed me most of the time. That says more about me than anything, but I'd never experienced not having a plethora of options to perfectly curate my little Christian community. Nevertheless, I tried to make the best of it and engaged, realizing this was a growth opportunity for me.

Late in that year, as the low-hanging fog of depression descended, the mix of constant work, strained community, and unavoidable isolation accelerated a drift away from God. The drift had started subtly a couple of months earlier, when the questioning and wrestling grew so tiring that I quit engaging.

Our transition back to the States was a whirlwind. We returned to Nashville, I took a job as an ER nurse, and we helped plant a church, an offshoot but separate entity from the church we grew up attending. We were already burned out from our time abroad and needed time, space, and rest to heal, but since church planting is not for the faint of heart, there was no time for any of that. So we did what we had always done as good Christians and churchgoers: we dove in headfirst. We showed up each week to set up and tear down equipment from the elementary school where we met, served in the children's ministry, led a small group, and filled in the various other areas that required time and attention, like one does when trying to nurture a baby church.

We were definitely not thriving; we were barely even surviving. Our three-year-old marriage was a mess—we were fragile, tattered, and worn thin. I was dying for an authentic community, somewhere with people who could bear witness to the pain of the isolation from our past year and the stress of what we had witnessed, people who could shoulder some of the burden. We were showing up on Sundays to do all the things, and I was even still spending time on my own with God, but I had never felt so spiritually distant from him or disconnected from myself.

Justin and I knew something had to give and finally called a truce. We were in a desperate place. We called up our pastor and told him we needed to take a break for a bit. Justin and I went away, separately, for a week at Onsite Workshops, a remarkable place that offers intense counseling and a space to heal and grow, with some of the nation's most highly trained and skilled therapists. We pulled out of our church commitments, knowing that we needed to just show up for a while without any obligations.

During this season the Enneagram reemerged for both Justin and me, in therapy and the personal work we were doing. We were first introduced to the Enneagram in high school. My sophomore year I began counseling for an eating disorder, and the Enneagram was part of the framework this group of counselors used with their clients. Initially I tested as a type One—all the boxes were checked and my behaviors matched the description. But after borrowing *The Enneagram Made Easy* from the bookshelf in my counselor's office and reading the chapter on type Eights, I felt like someone had peered into my soul and read my playbook. Without a doubt, I knew I was not a type One.

This is part of why I have never been a huge fan of Enneagram tests (an element of my type Eight-ness, of needing to push back, could also be at play here). Yes, they can be helpful and serve as a guide. But a test should be augmented by reading and dialogue with others to solidify your type. Mistyping is common, especially with a test, because most are not statistically validated and can naturally be so subjective.[1]

After confirming I was a type Eight, it was as if I had a new lens to see myself and my life through. I recognized that all the unhealthiest parts of me were on display, and the Enneagram ended up becoming instrumental in both my recovery and spiritual growth. Although I had "prayed the sinner's prayer" at a young age and grown up in the church, it wasn't until recovering from my eating disorder that my faith became my own. Through the work of relinquishing the control I craved and held tightly, I began to understand unmerited grace and experience the powerful work of redemption in my life. That was the beginning of my Enneagram journey, and this framework served as a guide as I grew, evolved, and engaged with others and the world around me.

The Enneagram became a prominent and powerful tool during our church hiatus, which turned out to be much longer than we'd imagined. However, something was different from when I'd first encountered it. I found myself discussing the Enneagram with the same enthusiasm and passion with which

I'd once discussed the gospel. Though I never wanted to hold the Enneagram, even with all its gifts, in higher regard than the Bible—the living, breathing Word of God—it felt more available, accessible, and tangible.

That's where some of us well-meaning and sincere Christians have gotten off track in this self-help-crazed world. I'm the chief offender in this. At times it's far easier to pick up a self-help book or listen to another podcast episode on personal growth than it is to open the Bible and dive in. That was the curse of the Enneagram on my spiritual life in that season. I reached for my Enneagram books more than I reached for my Bible. I talked more about types, wings, triads, and stances than I talked about the state of my spiritual life. Indeed, I was growing personally and relationally, but spiritually I was stagnant.

Justin and I began "looking at other churches," which translated into church-hopping on the Sundays it was convenient to go. Fall rolled in and with season tickets to the Tennessee Titans games, we didn't make it to church most weeks. We found a church we really liked but hung out on the fringes for a while, noncommittal and still somewhat skeptical. Once football season ended (sad but true) we began to regularly attend this new church and joined a small group of diverse, remarkable, and godly humans, but I remained hesitant. Deep down, I wanted things to be different. I had not envisioned myself ever being in this place and longed to find my way back—back home spiritually, back to the God I once knew and still believed in.

During those years, I strayed into a place of lagging and allowed myself to stay stuck in the unhealthiest characteristics of my Enneagram type and my sinful tendencies. Finally, when the pain of disconnection from myself and others had reached a fever pitch, I decided to take responsibility for my growth. I was sick and tired of being stuck spiritually and craved a tangible and practical catalyst that would lead me back to the heart of God. As I began to look for resources on personal and spiritual growth, specifically with the Enneagram, I found them to be few and far between. And what was available felt too cerebral and impractical, which left me wondering how to integrate the information into my everyday life. That is a big reason why you are holding this book right now.

The Risk and the Reward

Maybe some of my story resonates with you and you see threads of your own story in it, or you're standing in a similar place now—hesitant but willing and ready to take the next step. You know there has to be more; you feel it in your bones, even if your mind tries to rationalize otherwise. The feeling of not belonging, especially to the church or a Christian community, is perhaps some of the most exquisite pain one can experience as loneliness and disconnection compound. That risk of not fitting in or being rejected is very real, and though the stakes are high, so is the reward.

The reward of this spiritual Enneagram journey is that it is the road to rediscovering the God you once knew. To rediscovering the Jesus who met you that quiet night in the darkness of your dorm room, when you were entrenched in your eating disorder or crushed underneath the heavy weight of depression, and the only way out seemed to be the painless sleep of death. To uncovering those sinful tendencies that keep you trapped and stuck so you no longer have to be enslaved to or defined by them and can instead walk in freedom and wholeness.

In reconnecting spiritually and finding belonging with others—exactly where you are and for *who* you are—the reward is found. And on your journey to reacquaint yourself with the God you once knew, you may also encounter a God you have never known before.

3

ROAD MAP FOR
THE JOURNEY

DURING SPRING BREAK OF MY FRESHMAN
year of college, a car full of my sorority sisters and I headed for
the clear gulf water and white sand beaches of Florida. We printed
off directions from MapQuest from my dorm room printer. Yes,
that was back in the dark ages before iPhones, so you had to print
directions and pray they were right. Turns out they weren't, and
we got lost somewhere in Alabama, close to the Florida state line.
We stopped at a gas station and bought a map—a real map that
unfolds to the size of a newspaper, all the interstates and high-
ways snaking their way across the latitude and longitude lines.
We found out where MapQuest had led us astray and navigated
our way back to the highway that would take us to the shore.

Similar to my college MapQuest fiasco, where I realized
we needed an accurate map to get back on track, it would be
misguided if we jumped headlong into our spiritual journey of

building connection with God utilizing the Enneagram without a road map (the diagram below will serve as ours). This chapter will give you the definitions and tools to understand terms and movements associated with the Enneagram and each type. However, this chapter doesn't provide an overview of each type (that is in the chapters on individual types), so if you're still unsure of your type and want to start there, check out the resource section for test and book recommendations.

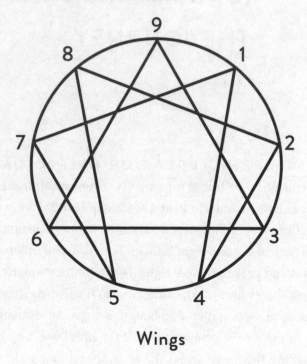

Wings

Let's start with the basics. Each person has one core Enneagram type. Because we are uniquely created, and factors like nature and nurture come into play, each individual is nuanced. It's not a cookie-cutter, one-size-fits-all kind of deal, and that's where the wing comes in. The term *wing* refers to the neighboring types that sit on either side of your number. Think of it like an airplane: the middle or body of the airplane, where the pilot and passengers sit, is your type, and then you have wings on either side. As a type Eight, I have a Seven wing and/or a Nine wing because those numbers sit on either side of the Eight. Most schools of thought with the Enneagram endorse the idea that wing types are the numbers on either side of your type, while some teachers say your wing type can be any other number. I'm in the camp that your wing is one or both of your neighboring types. This approach makes sense when you dive deeper into movement between wings in times of stress and growth, but it's not a hill worth dying on. So, whatever you think your wing type is, I won't argue with you over that. (I know, it's weird—a type Eight saying they won't argue?!)

Wings are simply expressions of your type. Think of them as your unique style or flare. For instance, there are several different kinds of citrus fruits—lemon, lime, orange, grapefruit, and so forth—yet they are all citrus fruits. Some people have very prominent wings, while others do not, and some have no wing at all. I have a friend who is a type Nine through and through. She has little to no Eight or One wing. If you've read about the wings that sit on either side of your type and neither one resonates with you, you may not have a wing.

Your wing isn't stagnant. It's entirely possible to vacillate between the two wings or to have lived most of your life predominantly with one wing and for that to shift over time. During my high school years, when I first learned about the Enneagram, it was apparent that I had a Seven wing. That Seven wing remained dominant through college and my early twenties, when I had no Nine wing to speak of. In my midtwenties, I felt a subtle shift away from my Seven wing and for a while I had no wing. As I approached motherhood and after my first son was born, my Nine wing burst onto the scene. This can happen over time as you grow and evolve through experiences and circumstances that bring out other sides of you.

Stress and Security

The Enneagram is not stagnant either; in addition to moving between wings, each type also moves to other types in times of stress and security.[1] You may have heard *stress and security* used interchangeably with *integration and disintegration* or *healthy and unhealthy*, but for the sake of our conversation we'll stick with *stress and security*.

Stress and security are represented by the intersecting lines on the enneagram (as seen on the diagram on page 22). Your stress type is where you gravitate when you're overextended, exhausted, or uncertain. For example, my husband, Justin, who is a type Three, moves to a type Nine in stress. This means that his typical high-energy, efficient way of engaging with life can slip into a slower pace, which sometimes looks like him procrastinating on a project or lounging on the couch to watch Marvel movies at four in the afternoon.

In terms of security, Justin moves toward a type Six. This makes him more methodical in his approach, asking questions and planning ahead instead of his usual quick-moving style: jumping first and building the plane as he's flying it, like type Threes tend to do. This move toward security happens when we are in a balanced state, stable, and generally feel safe. Refer to the chart on the next page and the enneagrams in each type chapter if all this movement talk is getting confusing.

TYPE	STRESS	SECURITY
EIGHT	FIVE	TWO
NINE	SIX	THREE
ONE	FOUR	SEVEN
TWO	EIGHT	FOUR
THREE	NINE	SIX
FOUR	TWO	ONE
FIVE	SEVEN	EIGHT
SIX	THREE	NINE
SEVEN	ONE	FIVE

Think of it like a continuum, a scale of 1–10. If you are in a healthy place with your thoughts and actions, you're functioning in the 7–10 range. If you are in an average space, you're functioning around a 4–6. If you are in an unhealthy place, you're functioning at a 1–3. This is where the terms *stress and security* or *integration and disintegration* can get tricky.

As a type Seven, my friend Kelsey goes to a type One in stress and a type Five in security. Over the years, she's done a tremendous amount of personal work in therapy and on her journey of faith. She is continually growing personally and spiritually; I'd say she typically functions in that 7–10 range. When she enters into a time of stress or moves to the type One, she doesn't automatically fall to the unhealthy end of the continuum just because she is stressed, although she certainly can. That would look like her being overly critical, rigid, and perfectionistic, but she can also move toward the healthy side if she is mindful and growing, acting disciplined, principled, and responsible.

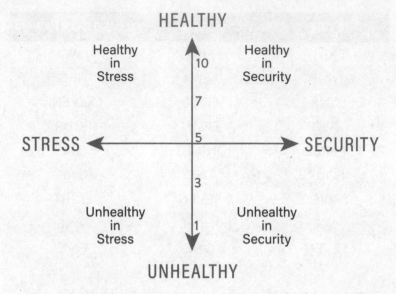

For a brief time in our early twenties, Justin and I worked in the emergency department at a level-one trauma center. There would be shifts when everyone's pagers were beeping, the radio was sounding with reports of five-minute ETAs, ambulances were pulling in, helicopters were landing, and all the trauma bays were filling up with patients who had been in car wrecks and were unresponsive or had sustained gunshot wounds to the chest, among other injuries. In those high-intensity and stressful (for any type!) moments, Justin would move to the type Nine. When this shift occurred, it was quite beautiful because he would spring into action, bringing unity and cohesiveness to a multidisciplinary team, all for the common purpose of providing the best care possible for a patient in a life-threatening situation. Using his wisdom and knowledge of people to diffuse internal and external conflicts and calm an otherwise chaotic situation, he accessed the high side of the resourceful type Nine in a healthy way, even in a time of stress.

Conversely, when he moves to a type Six in times of security, Justin can function in either the healthy or unhealthy range. If he were operating in that 7–10 range, this would look like him being responsible and reliable, leading from an altruistic place with courage, and trusting himself and others. However, even in a place of security (think relationships with a spouse, family, or close friends), he could fall to the 1–3 range, which would look like him overanalyzing to the point of anxiety, being codependent in relationships, and feeling fearful and distrusting.

It's important not to equate *stress and security* or *integration and disintegration* with being healthy or unhealthy. As mentioned earlier, some Enneagram educators use the terms *healthy and unhealthy* in place of *stress and security*. I intentionally do not equate *unhealthy* to *stress* or *healthy* to *security* because I think that creates a negative connotation, and the movement isn't always as simple as "healthy versus unhealthy." While these terms may correlate, that's far too narrow of a focus. The healthy-unhealthy continuum is a range, which is why this journey is dynamic rather than stagnant.

Triads

The nine points on the Enneagram can be further divided into three parts known as *triads*. The three triads are often referred to interchangeably as the *anger* or *gut* triad (types Eight, Nine, and One), the *shame* or *heart* triad (types Two, Three, and Four), and the *fear* or *head* triad (types Five, Six, and Seven). The triads delineate the core emotions of each type—anger, shame, and fear—and the body center from where they most reflexively see and operate: gut (or instinct), heart, and head.

Through the lens of spiritual growth, the triads and the core emotions each type experiences coincide with the suffering of each type. This suffering, as best as I can explain it, is simply the brokenness of our post-fall and pre-second coming existence. The emotions associated with each triad—anger, fear, and shame—are uniquely burdensome to their respective types. Furthermore, the sin tendency of each type compounds the suffering. We'll look deeper into what this means for each type and how it factors into one's spiritual journey in the chapters on individual types.

Sin Proclivity

You'll likely hear *sin proclivity* referred to as something slightly different across various books, teachers, and traditions. You may hear this element referred to as the *shadow side*, *vice*, *passion*, or *fixation*. For this book, since our focus is on one's spiritual journey, *sin proclivity* is the most fitting and appropriate as we explore each type.

TYPE	SIN PROCLIVITY
EIGHT	LUST
NINE	SLOTH
ONE	RESENTMENT
TWO	PRIDE
THREE	DECEIT
FOUR	ENVY
FIVE	AVARICE
SIX	FEAR
SEVEN	GLUTTONY

While "all have sinned and fall short of the glory of God" (Romans 3:23), for the purpose of spiritual growth it can be helpful to examine sins that may be particularly entrapping for your specific type. Reflect on your life and spiritual journey thus far. Is there a sin you tend to fall into more easily? Is there a temptation that seems to grab hold of your heart more tightly than others?

Above is an outline of the types paired with their specific sin proclivity.[2] If the sin proclivity paired with your type doesn't perfectly align with what came up when you reflected on your spiritual journey thus far, it may resonate more when we explore this in the coming chapters.

Virtue

The word *virtue* is derived from the Latin root *vir*, meaning "man," and the Latin word *virtutem*, meaning "moral strength, high character, goodness; manliness; valor, bravery, courage (in war); excellence, worth."[3] These days, we don't often hear the word *valor*, which *Merriam-Webster* defines as "strength of mind or spirit that enables a person to encounter danger with firmness: personal bravery."[4] Thinking of virtue in this sense powerfully positions the virtues of all the Enneagram types in the context of the world we live in, riddled with dangers and spiritual pitfalls that must be navigated with strength of mind and spirit.

In other words, the virtue of each type is its unique strength, tenacity, and energy. Spiritually speaking, these virtues reflect part of the character of God that we are able to embody and exemplify to the world, though only by his grace and because of the atoning work of Christ's death on the cross. These virtues don't necessarily correlate to our individual spiritual gifts, although there may be some resemblance. Similar to the sin proclivity of each type, we all embody all virtues. Just as we all fall prey to the sins associated with each type, we each have the ability, by the Holy Spirit at work in our hearts, to exemplify each of the virtues as fruits of the spirit.

Below is a table outlining each type's virtue.[5]

TYPE	VIRTUE
EIGHT	TRUTH
NINE	LOVE
ONE	PERFECTION
TWO	HUMILITY
THREE	HOPE
FOUR	ORIGIN
FIVE	TRANSPARENCY
SIX	FAITH
SEVEN	WISDOM

Essence

Essence is another term you will hear used interchangeably with a host of other terms in the Enneagram world: core, nature, soul, being. While many teachers and secular approaches speak of essence in more abstract terms, as a form of our true selves to be found and revealed, Suzanne Stabile put it simply and eloquently when she said at a workshop I attended that essence is "when Christ in me meets Christ in you."[6] From a spiritual perspective, the Christ in me and the Christ in you is the image of God that has been uniquely encoded into our DNA. As created beings, we reflect part of the beauty, magnificence, and uniqueness of our Creator, which shines forth through our essence. This will parallel beautifully as we dive deeper into each type in later chapters, but for now, here is a list of each type's essence.[7]

TYPE	ESSENCE
EIGHT	INNOCENCE
NINE	ACTION
ONE	SERENITY
TWO	FREEDOM
THREE	AUTHENTICITY
FOUR	EQUANIMITY
FIVE	OPENHANDEDNESS
SIX	COURAGE
SEVEN	SOBRIETY

Refer back to this road map as needed when you run across the different terms that have been defined and explained. As you read, you may feel compelled to skip ahead to your type or your spouse's, friends', family members', in order to understand them better. By all means, skip ahead. But then circle back. Remember that each type makes movements in stress and security and can vacillate between its wings, so you can glean and learn important things from every chapter.

From a spiritual perspective, my hope is that in each chapter ahead, practical applications will emerge as you walk your individual spiritual journey, rooted in biblical truths, growing in love and understanding for your fellow brothers and sisters in Christ, that we may all do as Paul admonished in Colossians 3:12–17:

> Put on then, as God's chosen ones, holy and beloved, compassionate hearts, kindness, humility, meekness, and patience, bearing with one another and, if one has a complaint against another, forgiving each other; as the Lord has forgiven you, so you also must forgive. And above all these put on love, which binds everything together in perfect harmony. And let the peace of Christ rule in your hearts, to which indeed you were called in one body. And be thankful. Let the word of Christ dwell in you richly, teaching and admonishing one another in all wisdom, singing psalms and hymns and spiritual songs, with thankfulness in your hearts to God. And whatever you do, in word or deed, do everything in the name of the Lord Jesus, giving thanks to God the Father through him.

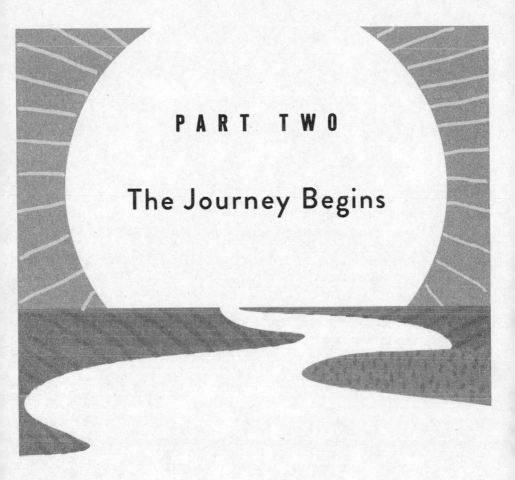

PART TWO

The Journey Begins

TYPE EIGHT:

TRUTH AND INNOCENCE

TYPE EIGHTS, ALSO KNOWN AS THE
Challengers (and my type), are natural leaders with the stamina to
scale to new heights and bring a refreshing, unadulterated truth
to the world. They are strong, self-confident champions who can
be unstoppable forces for justice and good when their energy is
harnessed and properly channeled. When an Eight enters the
room, they give off an energy that others inescapably notice.
Fiercely independent, protective, and passionate, they often see
themselves as invincible.

Often the most misunderstood of the Enneagram types,
these self-sufficient, boisterous beings are really kids at heart, but
their flagrant and unbridled anger can become a defense mech-
anism and a barrier to their growth. Spiritually attuned Eights
are able to stop relying on their anger and can step into their
virtue: speaking truth. But this virtue of truth emerges only

through vulnerability. Once they embrace healthy vulnerability, their childlike innocence and compassionate hearts enable truth to emerge in a soft and pure way instead of coming out in a pushy and steamrolling manner.

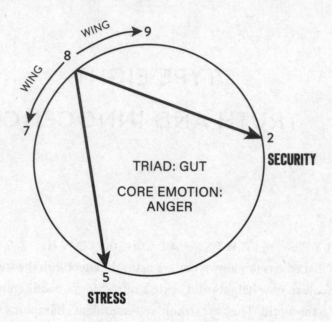

The Anger Triad

Type Eights find themselves in the anger triad, which adds a layer of complexity and energy to their sin tendencies of lust and vengeance. An Eight's anger is out, loud, and evident to them and others. Their anger is neither repressed as with type Nines nor turned inward as with type Ones. For type Eight, anger is visceral. They feel it in their gut and in their bones.

I've seen this anger present itself in my life many times. Once, as a three-year-old, I missed my best friend's birthday party because I split the back of my head open and was in the pediatrician's office getting a second round of stitches. To avoid the possibility of a flailing toddler who would likely injure herself more as she was being stitched up, the doctor and nurse secured me on a papoose board (they explained that it was like a skateboard without wheels with straps to hold me still). Imagine a kid lying facedown on a board with her arms and legs strapped to her sides to keep her from thrashing—that is a papoose board. Almost thirty years later, I still remember the shade of blue of the board.

I knew the drill from my prior experience with stitches: the more still I remained while they stitched me up, the quicker I could get back to playing. As young as I was, I did pretty well at the start, but I got to a point that I was done. "I'm getting hot—get me off this skateboard!" I yelled. I didn't have the linguistic skills to articulate that I felt vulnerable, but that was precisely what unleashed my anger at the medical staff.

Anger empowers the type Eight, making them feel strong and secure when they might otherwise feel vulnerable. When Eights find themselves in a vulnerable position, they will fight to their death to get out of it and use the energy from their anger to fuel the fight. Rather than leaning into an opportunity to trust, Eights take control so that they are not taken advantage of. When you understand that the tender heart of an Eight wants to establish trust but fears being betrayed, and is thus acting out to determine who is and isn't safe, this knowledge makes compassion for them a little more accessible (although it's still tough when their anger is so flagrant).

Eights' anger flares because trust feels as fundamental to their survival as water, food, and shelter, so they fight to find whom they can trust and then they fight to maintain that trust.

Though they're often accused of being on a power trip or being control freaks, it may surprise other types to learn that when Eights are functioning on the higher end of their type, they do not feel compelled to constantly be in control. But when they are in an unhealthy place, they absolutely fall into the trap of seeking control over people and circumstances. At their core, an Eight's desire is not to be controlled because being controlled puts them in a vulnerable position.

For Eights, the dominance of their control and destruction of their anger cause a lot of collateral damage. Like a tornado, their anger rages fiercely before it dissipates and the stormy skies are suddenly sunny and bright. The damage leaves those in its path reeling, while the Eight is done and ready to move on. However, the work for type Eights is not merely in tempering their anger but in trusting it.

The life's work of the Eight is learning to trust; a lack of trust is often the root of their outbursts. Therefore, trust is what allows them to relinquish their powerful grip on life, their plans, and the outcomes. But trust is not something to be conquered. You cannot accomplish it, master it, or check it off the life list once and be done with it. In the vernacular of a twelve-step program, step one, admitting you're powerless, is the step you return to throughout your life, at many times and in myriad ways. As journeymen in this lifetime, the hope is heaven, where we will one day be whole, healed, and home at last. Trust is the pathway, and vulnerability is the companion you must embrace if you desire the richness and reward to be found on this side of heaven. And along the way, you'll also be tasked with confronting the sin proclivity of lust, a process that can be the invitation into spiritual renewal for an Eight.

Sin Proclivity: Lust

More. More intensity, passion, control, power. That's at the heart of the sin proclivity of lust for the type Eight. Similar to type Sevens, Eights experience an all-consuming, insatiable, and ravenous desire for more. They become frantic with fervency, and their cravings lead to overconsumption (not just speaking of food or other substances here) when they live in an unchecked, uncontrolled, and crazed manner.

It's important to make the distinction between lust and passion for the type Eight. Eights are passionate people; that is part of their personality. But passion can turn to lust when Eights' desires go unbridled, their intensity is incessant, and their doing outpaces their thinking and feeling. Eights often confuse being passionate with having feelings, when in reality this excess energy masks emotion—especially the more tender ones, like fear and sadness—leaving them completely disconnected from their hearts.

One evening I was driving home after getting off a shift at the hospital, and I realized I was holding my breath. I was taking in shallow breaths that barely filled my chest, and my shoulders were tensed up near my ears. It had been a busy few weeks; in addition to working as a critical care transport nurse, writing, and being a mom, I was taking calls as a forensic nurse examiner and providing care to victims of sexual assault.

I was part of a small group of nurses in 2016 who established a Sexual Assault Forensic Nurse Examiner program to offer services to our city of Nashville. Since that time, the need for these services has continued to grow in the state, and in this particular week, I had spent several days traveling to train nurses at a rural hospital, helping them establish their own program to serve patients.

Even after long days over a couple of weeks, I still had a high, sustained energy level because of how deeply passionate I am about this work. But driving home that evening I thought, *I have not felt a feeling in at least three days.* That was a major red flag. The fact that I had to think long and hard about the last time I consciously felt an emotion was problematic. It clued me in that I was stuck in my head, disconnected from my heart, and running on passion while my feelings were inaccessible.

It's imperative in my work as a nurse that I have compassion, but I am able to be compassionate only when I access the softer emotions. Fear and sadness—which are harder and more painful for me to feel—are common in my work and the cases I see. When I am disconnected from my emotions, compassion isn't accessible, but when I am energized by my work, passion often looks like compassion. And it's easy for me to confuse the two.

Over the years this has become a red flag that alerts me when I need to stop and regroup. If I don't pause, breathe in through my nose, fill my lungs, and allow the emotions to emerge, I will keep charging ahead in life with passion. While passion is not bad and often contains the energy to bring needed and necessary change, in the type Eight passion in lieu of true emotion can come out sideways in excessiveness and spin up into lust.

Their lust for control creates the noose that type Eights will eventually hang themselves with if they are not spiritually attuned. For them, control is more important than connectedness, so they often find themselves isolated from community and spiritually estranged from God at their own doing. When they're spiritually derailed, they become aggressive, oppressive, and insensitive, indulging their lust by controlling their environment and the people occupying it. It can emerge in their workplace, when they feel like everything must be productive and purposeful or that the people involved are incompetent or not working hard enough.

Another way lust presents itself for Eights in their life and relationships is feeling as though everything must be meaningful or fun. "If there's a lull in conversation, I ask myself, *What's something funny we can laugh about?*" Annie, my sister-in-law, remarked. I've known Annie since she was two years old, and as fellow Eights, we often lament how our lust for more strains our relationships and inhibits our growth. "I find myself doing this regularly when I'm with family or friends because if we're not laughing, we'd better be having a deep conversation and if not, it feels boring," Annie went on to say. This lust shifts into a form of extremism when Eights believe that if things aren't interesting, productive, or purposeful, those around them (spouse, friends, family, coworkers) aren't doing enough.

When I'm slipping into a space of lust, it can look like boredom at the dinner table, where I find myself telling the most shocking or repulsive ER stories while using lots of colorful language. On a more serious note, I know I am careening off the side of the mountain when I begin to place unreasonable demands or expectations on those around me. For example, one time I insisted that my husband should be able to clean out the gutters, pressure-wash the deck, and haul trash to the dump before it got dark. The sun was setting in less than two hours and I pushed harder, until we ended up having a huge fight when he (very reasonably) expressed that he didn't think he'd be able to accomplish all that in such a short window of time. Not one of my prouder moments.

When Eights fall into the sin pattern of lust, everything is an overreaction, an overindulgence. It's on or off, all or nothing, in a not-so-helpful sense. Their lust is a general too-muchness, an obtrusive energy that they show up with when they are not actively drawing on the Holy Spirit to guide and temper them.

When Eights are barging along, they fall prey to believing that their lust is a helpful spotlight they shine on issues, bringing things into the light of truth to be addressed. But it's the exact opposite. Lust is their Achilles' heel. It's what will eventually destroy them. Eights will never lose their passion, but they need to surrender their unbridled and untamed energy. Eights, you don't have to be blinding and abrasive to be seen—you can still shine the light of truth, even with a dimmer.

Eights' energy, similar to their anger, is their kryptonite. If handled and channeled appropriately, they can change the world with it. But if misappropriated and converted into lust, it will destroy everything and everyone in its path. When the energy of their anger and lust converges, they can become fiercely vengeful, seeking to repay what is not theirs to repay, all in the name of justice. Romans 12:17–21 may as well have been penned specifically to every type Eight:

> Repay no one evil for evil, but give thought to do what is honorable in the sight of all. *If possible, so far as it depends on you, live peaceably with all.* Beloved, never avenge yourselves, but leave it to the wrath of God, for it is written, "Vengeance is mine, I will repay, says the Lord." To the contrary, "if your

enemy is hungry, feed him; if he is thirsty, give him something to drink; for by so doing you will heap burning coals on his head." Do not be overcome by evil, but overcome evil with good. (Emphasis added.)

Eights would do well to remember that less is more, bigger is not always better, and that simplicity and boredom are parts of life that cannot be escaped but rather should be embraced. This is imperative for the Eight who desires to be spiritually transformed.

"We always think the kingdom of God is 'out there'—it's something to go after, conquer, attain, and *do*, but most days it's here in my home, amongst my kids," my wise friend Hanna reminded me one morning as we sat on her couch with our babies. Hanna stands as a model to me of a powerful type Eight who has never lost herself. Her passion for teaching women the Word of God through her writing and speaking has never wavered, and she also has not allowed a lust for life and a desire for more to overshadow the beauty of the role of wife and mom in her current season.

Instead of continually charging ahead, arresting lust in its path will require Eights to slow down. When they do, what Eights often find is that so much of what they have dreamed of, hoped for, and worked toward is already here—they have it right now. Being grateful for those things and faithful in those roles is the responsibility of today.

Virtue and Essence: Truth and Innocence

The essence of the type Eight is childlike innocence. Many Eights identify with a childhood event or circumstance that caused them to lose their innocence, and they feel as though it was robbed from them. While some Eights may not have an event or childhood circumstance that caused them to feel this way, their lifelong battle with control, trust, and vulnerability positions them in a similar place. This loss of innocence may be something particularly important for them to explore in counseling with a trusted professional.

Spiritually speaking, this essence reveals the beauty of redemption. This innocence is a state of being unstained and unhindered by sin, free from all the pain and struggle that accumulates over a lifetime. It's the initial innocence of the garden, where Adam and Eve dwelt in Eden and communed with God, unencumbered by their vices, unashamed of their nakedness and vulnerability. Yet there's also a post-fall state of innocence that Eights can return to. Yes, innocence was lost with the deception of the serpent and the bite of the fruit, but it was found and restored with the atonement of the blood of Christ on the cross.

That innocence, of being declared not guilty and forever set free, is even more beautiful than the original innocence found in the garden. That's the goodness of redemption. The original state of sinless perfection isn't the most beautiful part: it's the new creation that we become after being washed in the blood. Jesus longs for the Eight to draw near to him—unhindered by their own facade of power and false sense of control—and experience communion with him and connection with others.

When type Eights set down their sword, relinquish their

death grip on control, and begin to embrace vulnerability, they can start to exhibit their essence of childlike innocence. In her book *Daring Greatly*, Brené Brown wrote, "Vulnerability sounds like truth and feels like courage. Truth and courage aren't always comfortable, but they're never weakness."[1]

Who's more fitting than the Eight to embody the virtue of truth, with their innate strength and courage cultivated from vulnerability? Perhaps it's the type Eight—on the pathway of vulnerability when they surrender from their striving and cease from their doing—who exhibits the virtue of truth to all the other types.

Truth and trust are inextricably connected for Eights. They need truth in order to trust, yet trust is what grounds them in truth. In the Old Testament, when God made a promise to Abraham, he entered into a covenant with him. As was customary during that time, when two parties established a covenant, they cut animals in half and walked together between the halves of these sacrificed animals. The act symbolized the importance of the covenant, that if either party broke the promise, what was done to the animals should be done to that person as a result of the breach of trust.

The closest we get to understanding the weightiness of a covenant in our day and age is when we enter into our own marriage covenant or witness a marriage. Even that, though it is of high importance and gravity, has become less significant over time, as so many marriages end in divorce. Covenants enacted and entered into by humans inevitably break. Trust is breached and betrayal erodes the promise made. However, covenants with God are a different matter entirely. In 2 Timothy 2:13 we're told that "if we are faithless, he remains faithful—for he cannot deny himself."

God doesn't need to enter into covenants. His promises are good; his word is true. But how gracious that he would enter into a covenant with us so *we* could be certain. Certainty is the crux of the matter for the type Eight. They *need* to know that they can trust. They need to know what to expect so they are not blindsided. Eights want the truth. The unaltered, non-sugarcoated, cold, hard truth. So let me shoot straight: Pain is impossible to avoid. Hurt will have a place in your story. Betrayal, real or perceived, will be inevitable. But you will survive it and live to proclaim the glories and wonders of he who created and sustains you, who guards and keeps you, who holds and protects you. Because he will never abandon or forsake you. Let your life be a testament to that truth of who God is. Be strong in the Lord and in the strength of his might, not relying on your own lustful, impassioned energy, but by trusting in Him. For when you are weak, then you are strong (2 Corinthians 12:10).

How to Grow as a Type Eight

Of all the types, Eights may be the hardest on themselves, with the exception of Ones. When emotionally checked in and self-aware, they can see the magnitude of the hurt their actions and anger can cause. They may seem unfazed, but internally they are berating themselves and beating themselves up. The spiritual growth path for an Eight doesn't mean ridding themselves of anger and passion but rather engaging appropriately with their energy. This keeps them from falling into the sin of lust and allows them to surrender control through vulnerability in order to connect with God. When Eights don't surrender through vulnerability to God and embrace vulnerability with others, they remain disconnected and isolated. To keep themselves out of sin and isolation, Eights must begin with the spiritual practice of stillness.

Stillness

Stillness for the type Eights arrests their constant *doing* and forces them to stop. *Pump the breaks* is something I remind myself to do often when my default setting of moving fast and furiously through life isn't helpful. In slowing down, I am able to listen, learn, and respond instead of react. Slowing down with the simple things—how fast I talk, how quickly I eat, and yes, even how fast I drive—creates a physical margin for stillness to enter.

"Trust in the LORD with all your heart," we are instructed in Proverbs 3:5. The irony of this, as a type Eight, is not lost on me. The energy of the Eight is visceral, and much of their time is spent in their head, thinking and strategizing, or relying on their gut instinct and responding accordingly. We type Eights may be more out of touch with our hearts than any other type; it's foreign territory that we don't often wander into because of its perceived perilousness. And yet we are told to trust in the Lord with all our *hearts*. Not trust in the plans we formulate in our heads, leaning on our own understanding. Not trust in the strength and stamina of our bodies or our gut instinct. The work of trusting, for the Eight, is what helps temper their energy, reconnects them with their hearts, and slows their hurried pace.

Finding stillness of body, as well as of mind and heart, helps buffer the reactiveness of responses for the type Eight. Stillness ratchets down their intensity so that they can connect with their heart and engage appropriately. Eights can begin to connect their body, head, and heart by breathing. Actually *feel* your lungs fill up with air on the inhale, then notice how it leaves your body on the exhale. Place your hand on the left side of your chest, over your heart, and feel the gentle rise and fall. Slowing down something as autonomic as breathing helps Eights connect with their heart and find internal stillness.

Journaling

Journaling about feelings is another important practice for Eights to become acquainted with the softer emotions that they often blow right past, hardly aware of their existence. This is where they get alone with God, allowing the gamut of emotions to arise.

Fear and sadness are two emotions the Eights can often substitute with anger. Anger has more energy and strength. It doesn't feel as helpless and scary as fear and sadness. But for personal and spiritual growth, it's important to become acquainted with other emotions.

Before going to bed, spend ten minutes journaling about what you felt that day, anger excluded. I know you think you didn't feel anything else, but that's the problem: you're *thinking*. Try to connect with your feelings; on your phone, set a few reminders throughout the day to pause, be still, and *feel*. You're wired to *do* and *think*, but stop and get acquainted with your heart and the feelings that are often inaccessible.

You can also incorporate prayer into your journaling practice. Prayer isn't merely a conversation between us and God—it includes seeking a place of solitude, getting still, being silent, and listening. Prayer requires a posture of humility to hear and receive what God has for us. With open hands, we can no longer grasp for control but offer up ourselves and our lives to God.

Here are a few journal prompts to use as a springboard:

- Where are you moving too fast right now in your life? Are you charging ahead when you may need to be slowing down?
- What are you afraid of in this season of life? Is there a circumstance that is causing you sadness? Journal about your fear or sadness and resist the urge to instead write about your anger.
- Open your hands, close your eyes, breathe in, breathe out. What do you need to relinquish control over right now?

Prayer and Meditation

Prayer and meditation, though they may feel painfully slow to the Eight, are vital practices in stillness. While I won't lie and say it's my favorite way to start the day, because it feels so counterintuitive to my mind and body, beginning the morning with stillness radically impacts the way I operate and the pace at which I proceed throughout the day. I *try* (and I say "try" because having a baby makes for an unpredictable routine) to begin each day with ten minutes of stillness and silence.

Practically, this looks like not reaching for my phone when I first wake up and instead getting out of bed and heading to the kitchen to make coffee. While waiting on the coffee, I resist a hundred urges to check my inbox, unload the dishwasher, tidy up, respond to texts—anything I could squeeze into the four minutes it takes for the French press to work its magic. Coffee in hand, I shuffle across our hundred-year-old hardwood floors to the yellow velvet couch next to the built-in shelves, where all my books are arranged in rainbow order. With the bright morning light streaming in through the windows on the east side of the house, I curl up on the couch, coffee balancing on the armrest, and set the timer on my phone for ten minutes.

For those ten minutes I practice stillness of body, mind, and soul. Sometimes I sit there with my eyes open; other times I lie down with my eyes closed and my body still. My mind inevitably wanders to the to-do list for the day, things I need to remember, but as quickly as they come, I practice releasing them, emptying my mind and bringing it back to a quiet place. Some days I'll choose a passage of Scripture to read over and over again. Other days I focus on one word. Regardless, this practice soothes my soul of the fear, franticness, anxiety, or anger that seek to overtake it. Sometimes it feels like an eternity has passed; sometimes it feels like I just sat down and found the place of stillness my soul was longing for, but either way, when the timer rings, I am centered and grounded. Physically, mentally, emotionally, and spiritually, meditation is extremely beneficial and it is so simple. But sometimes it's the simplest things that require the most discipline.

For type Eights, finding stillness of body, mind, and soul is paramount to their spiritual growth. In Psalm 23 King David paints a picture of where the Lord, as the good shepherd, longs to lead his sheep—especially the Eight: to lie down in green pastures and beside still waters, where he restores their souls. To find this physical rest for our bodies and spiritual restoration for our souls, Eights must be willing to slow their hurried pace of life, realizing that pushing rarely solves a problem and living fast and frenzied only fractures their connection with God and others. Still waters are the soothing scene and symbolic of the state Eights should seek.

REMEMBER

You will never be betrayed or abandoned by God.

READ

"Trust in the LORD with all your heart,
and do not lean on your own understanding.
In all your ways acknowledge him,
and he will make straight your paths." (Proverbs 3:5–6)

"But he said to me, 'My grace is sufficient for you, for my power is made perfect in weakness.' Therefore I will boast all the more gladly of my weaknesses, so that the power of Christ may rest upon me. For the sake of Christ, then, I am content with weaknesses, insults, hardships, persecutions, and calamities. For when I am weak, then I am strong." (2 Corinthians 12:9–10)

"And the LORD is the one who is going ahead of you; He will be with you. He will not desert you or abandon you. Do not fear and do not be dismayed." (Deuteronomy 31:8 NASB)

RESPOND

- The next time you feel impassioned or angered, before responding, exert some energy physically (for example, go on a brief walk or drop to the floor and do some push-ups). Burning off excess physical energy will help you engage in an appropriate and tempered manner instead of impulsively.
- Be quick to apologize *even if you weren't technically in the wrong*, especially when your energy is intrusive. If you realize this in the moment, stop and say you're sorry. If you realize after the fact, pick up the phone and make the call.
- Try living by the mantra "less is more." Let someone else have the last word, don't order a second drink, leave the emails in your inbox until tomorrow.
- Ask for help, even if you don't *need* it. You are highly competent and capable, but those characteristics can be a hindrance to vulnerability.
- When you must fight, let Ephesians 6:10–18 be your battle strategy and don't deviate from it.

5

TYPE NINE:
LOVE AND ACTION

TYPE NINES, KNOWN MOST COMMONLY AS
the peacemakers, embody love and unity and are one of the most
amicable of all the types. Type Nines are easygoing and provide a
reassuring, calming presence and stability when they walk into a
room. As true empaths, they genuinely see and understand each
person's perspective and pain. Their supportiveness is a powerful
propellant to any idea or endeavor. You're lucky if you have a type
Nine in your life.

The virtue that type Nines exhibit is love. Their love shines
brightest when they commit to showing up and engaging in
conversations and relationships that could cause either internal
or external conflict. The spiritual work of the type Nine is to
resist succumbing to slothfulness and instead take action that
promotes love and unity among humankind.

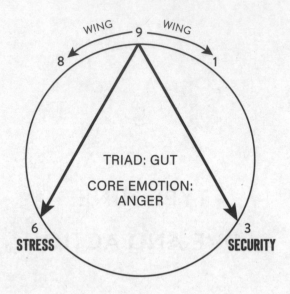

The Anger Triad

Type Nines are in the anger triad, which often goes unrecognized by themselves. When many Nines learn that anger is their core emotion, they think there is no possible way they are a Nine and therefore mistype themselves. One reason Nines are so unfamiliar and out of touch with their anger is because they are used to seeing anger expressed. Type Eights project their anger outward, making it easily visible, and type Ones turn their anger inward, which they can feel and others can sense. Type Nines repress their anger so deeply that its existence is just as surprising to them as it is to everyone else.

For Nines who have never been acquainted with their anger, sometimes somatic symptoms—neck pain, gastrointestinal (GI) upset, generally feeing unwell—can clue them in. "I always think I have food poisoning," said Courtney, a type Nine. "I've learned that's my body's response when I get angry and don't realize it."

On the occasions their anger does rise to the surface, it is quickly compartmentalized so as not to disrupt their life or anyone else's. Nines fear that their anger will be divisive. "Rather than ruining everyone else's day, I just keep to myself and ruin my day when I'm not in a healthy space," said Leah, another type Nine.

The triads can be confusing when it comes to the core emotions. Emotions aren't good or bad—they simply *are*. They are part of our human experience. Created in the image of God, we experience the range and fullness of emotions he—and Jesus, when he walked the earth as a man—experiences, though in their purest forms. We fallible humans can experience the shadow side of these emotions. The shadow side emerges when our emotions become distorted, when their original intent gets skewed, because circumstances make us feel as though something is true that may in fact not be. Instead of being a guide and an indication of something important, fear can become a fixation, shame can become toxic, and anger can fester.

There is so much well-meaning but poor advice derived from Ephesians 4:26–27, where Paul wrote, "'In your anger do not sin': Do not let the sun go down while you are still angry, and do not give the devil a foothold" (NIV). I have talked to more couples than I can count who were given the stern warning in premarital counseling to never go to bed angry with one another, with these verses referenced. If this verse were interpreted literally, some types would stay up fighting all night because going to bed without being angry is never going to happen. But contextually, it seems that Paul was imploring those at the church of Ephesus to resolve their anger quicky and not let it drag on and on rather than literally resolving their anger before going to bed. Unacknowledged and unresolved anger gives the enemy a foothold, providing him an opportunity to do what he does best: steal, kill, and destroy (John 10:10), which is why Paul stressed the importance of dealing with anger.

Anger feeds off self-pity and self-righteousness, which, for the type Nine, can translate into stubbornness and immovability, further compounding their sin proclivity of sloth. Selfish ambition and pride are anchor points of anger, leading to further entrapment and unwillingness.

Early one evening I sat on my porch swing with one of my dearest friends, Cassie—who is also my sister-in-law—as she recounted a story from the prior weekend, where she'd felt overlooked and unimportant. "I was so angry," she said somewhat casually, but it was not lost on me how much work it's taken for her to be able to say those words so matter-of-factly in a conversation.

A social worker by training, Cassie is a force for social justice, a fierce advocate for mamas and babies in her work as a doula, and a quiet but powerful presence of love. Her righteous anger for all the suffering and injustice in this world manifests through her passion and her work. "I feel so confident when I'm angry at something outside of myself," she has told me. But there is another layer of anger that had lain dormant in her for years. Having known her since middle school, I've witnessed it awaken in her in her adult years. "I truly never thought being angry was an option. I associated it with my goodness—that I'm a good person if I don't express anger, so I just cut it off. Even once I realized I was angry, I still had such a hard time opening myself up to it because it had been shut off for so long," she explained.

However, that anger has allowed her to awaken to herself, to her wants, needs, ideas, opinions, dreams—not just everyone else's. She resisted it, thinking that if she opened herself up to it, it would erupt and leave a wake of destruction in its path, ravaging all the peace she had strived to cultivate in her life, marriage, and relationships. But she came to find the exact opposite was true. In the instance we were discussing that evening on the porch, her awareness of her anger and having the courage to verbalize it to her husband enabled them to openly and honestly communicate with one another, strengthening their relationship and cultivating a deeper connectedness. "Even though it still kind of rattles me, I know it's okay. It feels like a foreign language that now I know a few words of, but it still feels strange," she remarked.

For type Nines, only once their anger is acknowledged can they then begin the process of no longer letting it fester and infect but instead channel it into energy that moves them to action. This is when anger can be a divine gift, bringing justice and good to a world filled with evil and suffering. When their anger is appropriately acknowledged and addressed, it prompts Nines to wake up, speak out, and take action.

Sin Proclivity: Sloth

The sin tendency of the type Nine, slothfulness, is not to be confused with laziness, because this type can be extremely hardworking. Slothfulness can present as preoccupying themselves with busy work, while procrastinating on doing what's important or avoiding it altogether. While this may seem relatively benign compared to the more overtly destructive patterns of the other types, Nines can live their days numbed out. This numbed-out, asleep state isn't truly living and leads to disconnection from themselves, others, and ultimately God.

The root of sloth for the type Nine comes from their innate need for internal peace. They desire to live settled and in harmony with themselves, others, and the world. While their desire for peace is pure, it can be overshadowed by indolence—aversion or avoidance. They live unfazed and unbothered by issues of great importance. In relationships, Nines will dodge almost anything that could infringe upon their peaceful state, which is why they are known to be conflict avoidant. This may mean that a marriage gets sacrificed on the altar of "keeping the peace" or a true friendship dissolves because the Nine avoids having the tough conversations. This can lead the type Nine to play roles shrouded in codependency, in the midst of big problems like familial dysfunction or addiction, and they numb out and avoid disruption. Coupled with the fact that Nines often throw themselves headlong into their vocational work or into caretaking roles to avoid their own personal and spiritual work, you've got a formula for dissatisfaction.

Type Nines will turn off alarms and ignore warning signs in their heads and hearts to maintain a perceived state of peace. It is merely perceived because peace derived from avoidance is not true peace. The problem or issue still exists; it just goes unattended, giving it time to smolder and cause further damage down the road. This can quickly and easily lead Nines down a pathway of resentment or cause them to act in a passive-aggressive manner.

Ecclesiastes 10:18 speaks to the dangers of sloth and indolence:

"Through sloth the roof sinks in, and through indolence the house leaks." A small leak in the roof may not seem like a serious issue at first, but if left unattended it can cause thousands of dollars in repairs, when a simple patch could have prevented further damage. For type Nines, the metaphorical roof leak (or literal roof leak in some cases) and their lack of attentiveness is not laziness. They avoid attending to the leak because it may lead to some kind of internal or external conflict, a state of dissonance. What if the leak is far worse than they think it is? What if it will require a whole new roof and they can't afford it? They are busy with other matters, so they put the leaking roof on their mental to-do list to attend to later, but later isn't a date on the calendar, so the roof goes unacknowledged until it is eventually altogether forgotten and ignored—or until the next big rainstorm reveals water dripping from the ceiling.

This sin proclivity of sloth also rears its ugly head when Nines neglect to do the personal and spiritual work required to grow. Growth is often uncomfortable, forcing us to confront unhealthy and sinful patterns by replacing them with new ones that are congruent with who we desire to be. "Slothfulness emerges for me when it comes to hard personal and spiritual work, like standing up for myself or for something that might involve discomfort, controversy, or rejection. It's just easier and safer to disappear," said Leslie, a type Nine.

Easier and safer, as Leslie described, is the path of least resistance for the type Nine. This perilous path leads them to place their needs on the back burner of their lives, avoiding and numbing, which causes them to disconnect. Nines disconnect from themselves by ignoring their needs and feelings, especially when their feelings might conflict with someone else's needs or feelings. Outwardly they may look in sync and connected with others, but in reality, they are going along to get along, merging their own ideas, thoughts, and opinions with others', which slowly builds resentment, anger, and disconnection.

"I love sleeping and rarely sacrifice sleep to get more work done," said Leah. Aside from an affinity for physical sleep, Nines can metaphorically fall asleep to their lives. Anything that could cause conflict, disruption, dissention, or encroach on their state of peace, they simply fall asleep to. If it's unpleasant, they stop thinking about it. If it's an opinion, they keep it to themselves. If it's disappointing, they pretend it's fine and never happened. This metaphorical sleep and even physical sleep can seem like a benign behavior from type Nines, but this is slothfulness masquerading as peace. Anything that allows type Nines to avoid thinking, feeling, or doing something that may cause disruption is a slow slide into slothfulness.

"Spiritual slothfulness has kept me from doing the hard work to appropriate the Lord's love for me, so I lived as a quietly crippled Christian for much of my life, believing in my head but not allowing his love for me, personally, to penetrate my own heart. Rather than fighting the enemy's lies, I invited them in and neglected my sword as it was too heavy, too unwieldy, for my weak arm to lift," Leslie explained as she beautifully articulated the core spiritual struggle of the type Nine. Believing the lie that their voice and presence do not matter, that they have no effect on the world, can cause Nines to slip into a state of spiritual slumber that is debilitating.

Virtue and Essence: Love and Action

While type Nines' mantra may be "good things come to those who wait," in actuality they would do well to heed the exact opposite. The essence for Nines, how they mirror Christ to the world, is action, which contrasts with their sin tendency of sloth. Type Nines have a bird's-eye view of the other eight types from atop the Enneagram, where they sit, seeing and perceiving others' needs, but the barrier they must overcome is in the *doing*.

It's through action that type Nines are able to love, wholly and fully, as they were uniquely created to do. Placating, perseverating, and procrastinating to avoid conflict or disruption is not kind or loving. True love, the virtue of the Nine, is backed by action— action in both the starting and completing. Some Nines have described this struggle with action using the concept of inertia: *an object in motion stays in motion*. Once they take action, they are able to continue, but getting started feels paralyzing at times.

It feels daunting to begin, and with all the mental stamina being consumed in their analyzing, Nines sometimes don't feel as though they have the physical energy for the task at hand. But once they start, it's easier to keep going than they imagined. Conversely, other type Nines enjoy the planning and the energy that comes with a new idea or endeavor but then quickly run out of steam, finding themselves with lots of good intentions that have become unfinished projects, unmet goals, and unfulfilled dreams.

When a type Nine pushes through the internal and external conflict, it can be world changing. As a Christian and white mother of two adopted black children, Courtney felt compelled to start conversations about race. While she knew this would create conflict, she began the conversations anyway. She was able to create a space where people could process their fears, ask questions, repent, or lament. Her powerful love for others drove her to action, even at the cost of creating conflict (and appropriately so) within her own community.

Type Nines strive for and are specifically gifted to seek internal peace and external harmony, but doing so is all for naught if they neglect the call to action rooted in love. True love is backed by action, and action is evidence of growing and flourishing faith, an idea reinforced in James 2:14–17:

> What good is it, my brothers, if someone says he has faith but does not have works? Can that faith save him? If a brother or sister is poorly clothed and lacking in daily food, and one of you says to them, "Go in peace, be warmed and filled," without giving them the things needed for the body, what good is that? So also faith by itself, if it does not have works, is dead.

Or as Leah explains,

> A person who follows through with what I say, who meets the needs of others before they're spoken, who goes above and beyond, who accomplishes goals instead of just dreaming about them, that's the person I aspire to be. It doesn't come easily or naturally, but in my mind, that is my "ideal self." That is the person I know I can be when I'm growing in my relationship with Christ.

This is the beautiful state of what is not only entirely possible but probable when Nines engage and act; it is their faith in action and love on display for the world to see.

The idea of love feels natural and is ingrained into the type Nine but getting there through action can feel like an overwhelming obstacle, leaving them uncertain of where to start. That is where the work of growing in the virtue of love presents itself. Oftentimes we like to make things more complicated than they really are, but sometimes it's the smallest steps and simplest practices that propel us the furthest. Love is often a lot of little things—those small, repeated actions over time that, in the end, become big things.

My sister Jordan, a type Nine, has done remarkable work at establishing a morning routine that sets the trajectory for her day. She wakes up at 5:00 a.m., drinks coffee while she reads her Bible and writes in her journal, works out, and eats a good breakfast before starting work. There is nothing revolutionary about her routine, but it is a series of physical actions that function as the springboard for her soul to awaken to the day.

How to Grow as a Type Nine

Nines spend an enormous amount of energy mitigating, mediating, and managing the needs and emotions of others as well as their own, which is why they may find themselves physically exhausted, seeking places and times of relaxation and peace. While type Nines may often find themselves physically still, there is rarely a state of stillness in their hearts and minds. The spiritual practice of stillness for the type Nine is nuanced because it is not necessarily physical stillness they need but an internal stillness that brings them into an awakened state of alertness and engagement.

Stillness
Stillness paves the way for type Nines to actively engage in their relationship with God and relationships with others, illuminating the gift of love and peace they bring to the world. The type

Nine who has awakened, engaged, and expended their energy on their personal and spiritual growth is a vessel of light and love in action in a dark and hurting world.

Throughout the New Testament, Paul repeatedly admonished the church to wake up from their spiritual slumber and get to work:

> The commandments . . . are summed up in this one command: "Love your neighbor as yourself." Love does no harm to a neighbor. Therefore love is the fulfillment of the law. And do this, understanding the present time: The hour has already come for you to wake up from your slumber, because our salvation is nearer now than when we first believed. (Romans 13:9–11 NIV)

Salvation, the return of Christ, is nearer than when we first believed, and there is much work to be done. The first part of that passage from Romans comes easily to type Nines. Loving others is instinctual for them. But true love—love that is selfless, not self-forgetting, sacrificial, not self-abdicating—is possible only when they are awakened. This state of awakening for the type Nine, where their love for others turns into action—especially when that action may cause dissonance or conflict—is powerful and pure.

Physical movement helps Nines practice spiritual stillness. Although it seems counterintuitive, physical movement brings a stillness of mind and soul that allows them to awaken. If you are a Nine, try going for a walk and rather than let your mind be empty, awaken it by focusing on a specific word or meditating on a passage of Scripture.

Journaling

Journaling about your wants and needs is extremely helpful in homing in on what you feel and think—often things that you or others have dismissed, deeming them unimportant. Find a quiet place (not while you are listening to a podcast or have a show playing in the background) and journal about those wants and needs. It may take time for them to rise to the surface, but remain alert and attentive; they're there and they will arise. Once you identify your needs and desires, consider allowing others to love you by meeting those needs and desires. I know: you're worried you'll be a burden, plus it might rock the boat if you verbalize them. But you've likely sufficiently minimized their importance already. They matter and *you* matter. Allow others the privilege and gift of loving you. Not asking for what you want and need, or for help, robs others of the joy of loving you, being kind to you, and being there for you. You aren't "helping" by closing yourself off to support or disallowing others to help you.

While journaling about your needs and wants, take time to process things that you are not directly confronting someone about. Release what you've been holding: sadness, fear, hurt, and anger. Work through it instead of avoiding it. You may find clarity on conversations you need to have and build the courage to do so.

Pull out your calendar (get one or download an app if you don't have one) and schedule time for your spiritual growth. Spiritual disciplines take time to ingrain into your daily life but they will compound into something powerful over time, if you practice them consistently. It's okay to schedule them into your day. After all, you do that with anything else you prioritize. It won't just happen overnight; you have to work at it each day. If there's not a deadline or date, it's not a goal—it's a dream that may never materialize. Turn it into a S.M.A.R.T goal (specific, measurable, attainable, realistic, timely).[1] Instead of saying, "Have a more consistent quiet time," change it to "Read the Bible for fifteen minutes every day." Add reminders to text someone or call them to meet for lunch or coffee instead of half-heartedly saying, "Let's get together soon."

Do a brain dump at the end of each day, writing down what you didn't get done today and what you need to do tomorrow. If you didn't get to a task, errand, or chore, write it on a sticky note and post it on a physical calendar, on the date when you will do it later. This will decrease the overwhelming panic that may arise, allowing your mind to rest.

You may find the following journal prompts helpful in your journey of spiritual transformation:

- What habits are you holding on to that don't serve you? Are there more beneficial habits you could choose instead?
- Is there something you've been putting off that needs to be dealt with? Process through it and then decide a date when you will act.
- Is there a person in your life you are harboring resentment toward or have been acting out in a passive-aggressive manner toward, even subtly? What steps do you need to take to acknowledge the issue, release your resentment, and make amends for any passive-aggressiveness on your part?

Ground Yourself in the Present

Ground yourself in the present by bringing stillness to your mind, body, and soul. Release your mind and body of all the managing, mitigating, and mediating. You carry that with you always, and it's a heavy and exhausting load. You may feel where this weight shows up physically, in your tense shoulders, stiff neck, or upset stomach. Let the past rest; let the future take care of itself. "Sufficient for the day is its own trouble," Matthew 6:34b reminds us. Be present to yourself so that you can be present to others, allowing love to flow forth.

Be aware of slothfulness that may be masked as stillness. Rarely will sleeping an extra hour in the morning, vegging out after work, or watching another show bring the stillness needed to energize your soul. Much energy is required to know yourself and know God, but he is sufficient and will supply every need, including the physical energy required for the day and the task at hand.

"Tell me, what is it you plan to do with your one wild and precious life?" Mary Oliver penned in her poem "The Summer Day."[2] This is the question for Nines: What will you do? And then *go do it*. Show up to your life. It is a wild adventure waiting to unfold, but you must be present and actively participate in it. Once you have awakened to the adventure, you can then fully and wholly show up to love others. They will never be able to experience the divine love you are capable of giving them if you wait for the perfect opportunity, when the waters seem settled and peace feels promised.

REMEMBER

You matter and your voice matters.

READ

"I have said these things to you, that in me you may have peace. In the world you will have tribulation. But take heart; I have overcome the world." (John 16:33)

"'Awake, O sleeper,
 and arise from the dead,
    and Christ will shine on you.'
Look carefully then how you walk, not as unwise but as wise, making the best use of the time, because the days are evil." (Ephesians 5:14b–16)

"Love is patient and kind; love does not envy or boast; it is not arrogant or rude. It does not insist on its own way; it is not irritable or resentful; it does not rejoice at wrongdoing but rejoices with the truth. Love bears all things, believes all things, hopes all things, endures all things." (1 Corinthians 13:4–7)

RESPOND

- Be mindful of slothfulness that may be masked as self-care: watching one more Netflix show episode, unplugging by mindlessly scrolling on Instagram, or taking a hot bath with a glass of wine that turns into half the bottle.
- Pay attention to the moments in conversations and social settings when you zone out. Spend time thinking or journaling about why you zoned out or disengaged.
- What are you procrastinating on or putting off? If the task takes less than five minutes, do it right now.
- When asked, voice your opinion or idea. Better yet, volunteer it without being prompted.
- Actively participate in the relationships in your life. Your presence matters tremendously, and the rest of us miss out on the glory of you when you sink back, zone out, or disappear.

6

TYPE ONE:
PERFECTION
AND SERENITY

THE TYPE ONES, COMMONLY REFERRED TO as the reformer or perfectionist, keep the rest of us and the world from completely derailing, with the high ideals, morals, and ethics they conduct themselves and lead with. Highly responsible and virtuous, with a default operating mode of integrity, Ones are constantly self-reflecting to see how they can better themselves while also seeking opportunities to better their sphere of influence.

Ones see the world—and all that's within—through the lens of holy perfection: the way it was created to be and will become again with the second coming of Jesus Christ. But in the in-between time, serenity is what they manifest when they are able to actively seek what is good and right, while concurrently holding the tension of all that is wrong in this world.

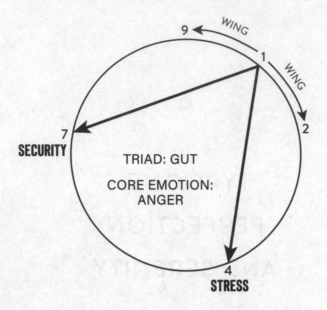

The Anger Triad

The low boil of resentment compounds the anger Ones already feel. Whereas type Eights express and externalize their anger and Nines ignore its existence, type Ones aim to control and suppress their anger because in their estimation, it is "not good."

Similar to Nines in some respects, Ones have a complicated and confusing relationship with anger. While we all know the feeling of righteous anger and outrage, I'm willing to bet Ones know it more intimately and viscerally than the rest of us because of the lens through which they see the world: good and bad, right and wrong, black and white.

"I harbor and hold on to resentment, smoldering over someone's incompetence or even my own incompetence/failure in something but try not to show it because that's not the 'right' thing to feel. But it all sits there like acid in my stomach," explained Jordyn, a type One. Unless it's for a righteous cause, Ones keep their anger bottled up because of their belief that it is not good. "We suppress our anger and convince ourselves we're not angry, which turns into judgment, envy, resentment, and bitterness," Caleb, another type One, told me.

Ones suppress their anger not only because they believe it is not good but also because they fear that *if* they express it, they may explode from all the built-up pressure that has accumulated over their lifetime. They keep their anger in check so that it doesn't come out inappropriately or at an inopportune time.

But holding on to it comes at a cost. Our bodies retain the emotions that we are either unaware of or unwilling to express in healthy ways. Anger oftentimes manifests in the body in the form of chronic headaches and neck soreness, a clenched jaw, teeth grinding when sleeping, or in various stomach issues, feeling like there's a huge knot or general uneasiness. Ones, if you have suppressed your anger to the point of truly believing you are not angry, tracing the anger and first connecting to it somatically can help you become aware of it. As you notice these somatic responses, connect that with your head. Ask yourself, *What am I thinking about?* Once you have moved from the somatic to the cerebral space, connect to your heart and enter into the feelings space, where you'll tap into your anger. And as much as you may have been raised to believe or internally held on to the belief that feeling anger is "bad," I'm here to tell you it's okay.

Ones sometimes get a bad rap for being overly critical and judgmental of others. If they had a hashtag, it would be #dobetter or #detailsmatter. But realizing the weightiness of what they carry should prick our hearts with tremendous compassion for them. Each of us has an inner critic, but type Ones never get a break from theirs. Their ruthless inner critic uses a megaphone to incessantly broadcast their shortcomings and mistakes.

They have extremely high standards and ideals, and although it feels like it sometimes, they aren't trying to be nitpicky. Good enough is just never good enough. The dishes weren't loaded correctly, there were missed typos in the email newsletter, someone canceled so they had to pick up the slack. Nothing is done quite right, so they go behind and fix it all, commenting and critiquing so the rest of us will be aware for next time.

Living with that low threshold for failure, feeling like you must take care of things and clean up the mess because it's the "right thing to do" would make any of us feel angry. Ones, if no one has ever told you this, know that your anger is not bad—it is not wrong, it is not a sin. You probably picked up that message early in your childhood, and it's a narrative you'll need to unlearn in order to grow.

Anger is a normal part of the human experience, and it can be good even though it doesn't *feel* that way. Your anger is alerting you to something that needs correcting. Yes, it can take a wrong turn if it is ignored and repressed and seep out as resentment. But anger and the energy that comes with it can be a catalyst for change. Anger is part of the process of sanctification and transformation for yourself and for the world.

Sin Proclivity: Resentment

"Up at daylight trying to rid the world of injustice" like eight-year-old Fern from *Charlotte's Web*,[1] type Ones are on a crusade to eradicate the imperfections of the world, right all the wrongs, and clean up the terrible mess. It's unbearable and overwhelming for them to witness the evil, wrong, sin, and darkness that runs rampant, and they feel a constant compulsion to do something about it. They feel responsible and will act accordingly, even when those who may be responsible will not.

Though their desire to right the wrong is good and their efforts are noble, they can slip into a state of resentment if they are not cautious and aware. Continually falling short of perfection leaves Ones with a permanent, low-level frequency of frustration. People are not how they should be, and they don't do what they are supposed to do. Nothing is as it's supposed to be—life is not what it should be.

That's the catch-22: Ones are right. Life is not what it should be. It's not fair, it's not right, and it's not supposed to be this way. Perfection no longer exists on this earth since the entrance to Eden was barred, and that is where Ones' resentment is born.

There is a deep chasm between how things are supposed to be and how they are. Ones feel the crushing weight of disappointment from the expectation of how things were designed to be and the reality of what they are. But instead of holding that tension and finding peace in the imperfection until all the wrong is finally made right, their anger takes on a passive-aggressive edge and morphs into resentment. Living under the weight of all the "shoulds" and "not supposed tos" becomes unbearable and infuriating, causing the bitter indignation of resentment to take root in their hearts.

Being critical is one of the ways that resentment surfaces. Type Ones are critical of themselves, others, and everything around them, constantly seeing what is wrong, what can be improved on, and what isn't good. Instead of a simple "oh hey, by the way . . ." approach when something wasn't done correctly, type Ones can erupt with criticism seemingly out of nowhere.

Jordyn explained, "Coming home from work one day, I found

that my husband had folded the laundry, emptied the dishwasher, and prepped the coffee pot for the next morning. And you know what was the first thing that came out of my mouth? 'Hey, Jon, you spilled coffee grounds on the counter. Can you clean this up?' No 'thank you' or appreciation. I skipped over all the great stuff he had done and jumped to the *one* wrong thing I could find."

When not in check, this critical outlook can be extremely damaging to others as well as to type Ones' souls. When their critical mindset takes over, Ones no longer see the inherent good in God's creation, the way the world and all of creation was in Genesis 1 and 2. To combat the core of criticism, type Ones need to be reminded that even if the circumstances aren't good, God is still good and he is for their good. Focusing on God's sovereignty, seeing that seasons of change are a part of life, and reminding yourself that it won't be this way forever helps you trust the process and trust that God is still working, even on the slow and painful path of transformation.

On a practical level, curbing their critical tendencies begins with delegating tasks and allowing the delegate to carry out the task as they see fit. As a mom of five and a type One, Kimmy said that "unless it floods the kitchen or causes a catastrophe—real, not perceived—the kids get to load the dishwasher whatever way they want." Ones, unless it creates a safety issue (again, real not perceived), instead of stepping in and saying something, let someone take a task off your plate and accept the help, because you could surely use it. You might have a tendency to want things your way, but growth happens when you encourage instead of criticize, even if the dishes could have been loaded more efficiently.

In the Ones' endeavor to restore order, right the wrongs, and reestablish good where things have gone awry, they can slip into perfectionism. Not to be confused with a healthy striving for excellence, which has its place and appropriateness, perfectionism is a dead-end road. The pursuit of perfection has only two destinations: pride or despair. Pride because we are above and better than, or despair over where we fall short. It's seeing what we have been giving as insufficient and lacking. Striving for perfection is also a subtle way of rejecting what God has created and given, has stamped with his seal of approval as good. Resentment communicates a lack of trust in God and his plan. Rather than resenting, the work is in surrendering control, believing that the work isn't finished yet, and trusting in the greater plan and in the process.

Yes, the world is stained by sin. But what God created and said was good is still good. Although it's no longer perfect outside the barred gates of Eden, the goodness is not diminished. Perfection isn't the point. Atonement—reparation of wrong—was completed once and for all on the cross, and perfection is our hope for what is to come. Meanwhile, good enough can, in fact, be good enough. Good enough is what we have in the here and now while we await the second coming of our Savior, and there is peace to be found in that.

Virtue and Essence: Perfection and Serenity

If ever a type could live out Paul's words and spur the rest of us on to do the same, it's the Ones of the world:

> Not that I have already obtained this or am already perfect, but I press on to make it my own, because Christ Jesus has made me his own. Brothers, I do not consider that I have made

it my own. But one thing I do: forgetting what lies behind and straining forward to what lies ahead, I press on toward the goal for the prize of the upward call of God in Christ Jesus. (Philippians 3:12–14)

Ones who are spiritually attuned, not falling into futile striving but with their eyes fixed on the prize, are powerful catalysts to the rest of us in our own journeys of sanctification. Ones spur the other eight types—who may otherwise be comfortable with "good enough" and bail out on the work of refinement and transformation that God wants us to do. That is when the Ones' mentality—good enough is never quite good enough—can serve the rest of us well. Our sanctification is never a matter to settle for, and Ones are rarely able to settle.

Ones will have to grapple with "good" and "good enough" to find serenity. In Genesis 1 and 2, everything was *good*—it was *very good*. Then, if you skip to the end of the Bible and read Revelation 21 and 22, all is made new—the work of redemption, sanctification, and transformation is done; it is finally finished. But we are living in the unholy and imperfect time between Genesis 3, the fall of man, and Revelation 18, when the old earth will pass away. If any type feels the burden of this in-between time and clearly sees the ravaged and wretched world we live in as a result of sin and darkness, it's the Ones.

The work for a One is to make peace with all that is wrong, broken, and dark in this world. I know that makes you Ones shudder. But I said *make peace*, not let go, not let be, not be okay with. Making peace will mean realizing and then embracing the fact that we live between Genesis 3 and Revelation 18. God's kingdom is here and now, yet there is plenty of work to be done—and Ones are likely spearheading the charge. But this side of heaven, the work will never be finished, and the wrong will not be made right. Though it will in time, we're in the messy not-yet and the painstaking in-between. And that is what you must make peace with, Ones.

Accepting imperfection as a pathway to peace is the journey Ones must willingly subject themselves to in order to experience transformation and find serenity. All that is wrong and sinful in the world, that is not as they would have it, is what paves the way to serenity, because it requires them to trust that he who began a good work in them (and in this terribly messed-up world around them) will bring it to completion—the completion set forth in Revelation 21 and 22.

Serenity comes with surrender. This is not an apathetic, throwing-in-the-towel, "I don't care anymore" sort of act but rather a surrender to the sovereignty of God. Reasonable happiness, to use the twelve-step verbiage, is all that is possible in this life in the "now" and "not yet." Supreme happiness, which for Ones is actual perfection, is possible only in the next life. When Ones make peace with imperfection, they manifest serenity to the rest of the types. Believing that everything has been made beautiful in its time (Ecclesiastes 3:11), even in and especially amid its unfinished imperfection, Ones encourage others on their journey homeward, pressing toward the prize with peace and patience in the process.

How to Grow as a Type One

Stillness

The spiritual work for the type One is to cease from their perpetual state of doing—of working to right the wrong, to bring justice to the injustice, and to restore order. For the type A, high-strung, stressed-out, overworked, overwhelmed, and worried Ones of the world, stillness isn't a familiar state. Though counter-intuitive to their energy and drive, stillness makes the path to peace with imperfection possible. Stillness helps Ones engage in rest, providing a much-needed place of reprieve for their weary souls. The journey of transformation and process of sanctification will never be fast enough for you Ones, but choosing to be still, instead of spinning your wheels by constantly doing, will ironically speed up the process.

Practicing Gratitude

Practicing gratitude is transformative for Ones because it requires them to actively choose thankfulness in the mess. Acknowledging the good before criticizing is where being thankful starts. Guided gratitude meditation, gratitude journals with prompts, or even the act of jotting down five things you're thankful for at the end of the day shifts the focus from what's wrong and imperfect to what is *good*. This is a grounding practice for Ones that will keep them rooted in contentment.

Ones, instead of focusing on what you can't control, what isn't being done, or what's being done wrong, gratitude will help you see what you *can* do and focus your efforts appropriately. Sometimes what you can *do* is simply pray and practice thankfulness in all circumstances. Gratitude is a gracious companion that you'll want alongside you on the long and nonlinear journey of transformation. You are great at identifying the problem, finding the solution, and making a plan to accomplish what needs to happen, but the painful process of sanctification is where gratitude will guide you into a place of peace.

Journaling

Journaling is a powerful practice for Ones because, by the very nature of the activity, it forces them to focus on one thing instead of multitasking. Additionally, the tactile component of pen to paper slows down both the body and mind, allowing them to better access their hearts. Ones, find a spot in your home—a comfy chair in a little nook, the kitchen table with the morning light streaming in—where you can sit and be and write, processing what you're thinking and accessing your feelings. Jordyn said, "Some of my biggest 'aha' moments and life-shaping decisions have come from journaling. Stopping long enough to realize what I'm actually thinking and feeling *and* stopping long enough to realize what God has been trying to say all along."

As you journal, take some time to ask yourself a few questions:

- What resentments have I been harboring? Can I trace this tension to a place in my body? What is blocking me from releasing it?
- In this season of life, what lesson am I learning that I am grateful for?
- Write a letter to your inner critic. Be curious about its origin, when you first became acquainted with him or her. Ask what they are trying to protect you from. What are they wanting you to know or do? Thank them for how they are trying to help, but let them know you've got this and don't need their constant criticism.

Being in Nature

Being in nature, a place of untamed wildness that is perfectly designed by God, helps bring inner peace and calm to the swift cadence of the One. Nature is the ultimate reminder that we are not in control; we do not have the power to silence storms, stop tsunamis, or call the sun forth from the clouds. Nature and its serenity offer Ones an environment for simply *being*.

Being Versus Doing

Spending time *being* rather than *doing* is of paramount importance for the One. In her book *Walking on Water*, Madeline L'Engle wrote, "When I am constantly running there is no time for being. When there is no time for being there is no time for listening."[2] Ones easily fall into the trap of doing, including doing a lot for the Lord: leading small groups, heading up community initiatives and service opportunities, and volunteering their time, skills, and expertise. But when they get sucked into the doing, they miss the relationship that comes from just being together, simply talking and listening.

What makes being and listening particularly challenging for the type Ones is that during these times, their harsh and relentless inner critic often arises, badgering and berating them. Who can blame them for keeping busy, watching shows and listening to audiobooks or podcasts while carrying out daily activities like cooking, cleaning, and household chores, which would otherwise be great opportunities to practice stillness of soul and listening? But that's where the work lies—in choosing the practice of being and listening, and not letting that inner critic have the final say. Listening to the soft and gentle voice of Jesus, which speaks truth and grace and love. Intimacy is experienced in being with the Lord, and the practice of stillness is what draws the One's heart to God. The philosophy of idle hands being the devil's workshop could not be further from the truth for Ones.

In fact, constant motion is the anthesis of what type Ones need in order to experience transformation. Transformation takes time. It's not linear like we might wish. It's in the stopping, slowing, and stillness that the work of transformation is carried out in their hearts.

Accepting Reality

Although the process of accepting reality can be painful at times, it propels Ones along their growth trajectory. Ones straddle the space of being both a realist and an idealist. Because they see all that is wrong yet have a clear vision of what the world can be, their work is in acknowledging and accepting the current reality rather than taking action to bring about the ideal.

In acknowledging and accepting reality, Ones, you should know that you're probably right. You give the "right" advice and you often know the "right" answer, the "right" thing to do. But people don't always follow the advice you give, even when they asked for it, and they don't do the "right" thing. Unfortunately, that is something you must make peace with. Growth happens in those times when you can stay in a place of humility instead of slipping into pride (even though you were right!), by extending grace to others. Your integrity feels like it is inseparable from what is right, but walking in humility doesn't diminish your integrity. People are in process, and *you* are in process—give yourself a break and give others a break too. When you become too practical, you become less personal. Sometimes relationships are more important than rules.

REMEMBER

You are good, and good is good enough.

READ

"So speak and so act as those who are to be judged under the law of liberty. For judgment is without mercy to one who has shown no mercy. Mercy triumphs over judgment." (James 2:12–13)

"For thus said the Lord God, the Holy One of Israel,
 'In returning and rest you shall be saved;
 in quietness and in trust shall be your strength.'"
　　(Isaiah 30:15)

"But he said to me, 'My grace is sufficient for you, for my power is made perfect in weakness.' Therefore I will boast all the more gladly of my weaknesses, so that the power of Christ may rest upon me." (2 Corinthians 12:9)

RESPOND

- Spend your daily commute in prayer and reflection. This is built-in time to just *be*. You can't be checking things off the to-do list or doing the things you otherwise *should* be doing during this time.

- Keep a little notebook close by and when you make a mistake, write it down and then let it go. This simple and seemingly silly practice can help you begin to embrace the grace that is waiting to wrap its arms around you.

- Pay attention to the areas of your body that are constricted. Is your neck sore? Are you clenching your teeth? Does your stomach feel upset? Relax your shoulders, loosen your jaw, put your hand gently over your belly and breathe deeply.

- Schedule a self-care activity. Your constant doing doesn't make you deserving of a break. Realizing that rest isn't selfish is a mindset shift you'll need to make. After all, rest was one of the earliest ordinances in the Bible (see Genesis 2:2).

- Notice the nuance between perfection versus preference in your life and in the lives of others. Your standards, ideals, and views on a matter aren't necessarily wrong, but they may not be "right" either—perhaps they are merely your preference.

7

TYPE TWO:

HUMILITY AND FREEDOM

TYPE TWOS, KNOWN AS THE HELPERS OR givers, are deeply loving, incredibly caring, and profoundly compassionate. Their warm countenance and approachableness, paired with their nurturing energy and patience, creates a magnetic pull for others toward them. Easily perceiving the needs of others, they exemplify biblical servanthood unlike any other type through their generous love and sacrifice for others.

The virtue of the type Two is humility, which is displayed most beautifully when they are living out Philippians 2:3: "Do nothing from selfish ambition or conceit, but in humility count others more significant than yourselves." When they are able to recognize their own worth, needs, and desires first, attending to and honoring them, then they can truly give of themselves in selfless service to others, reflecting the heart of Christ.

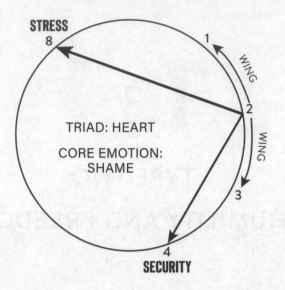

STRESS
8

1

WING

2

WING

TRIAD: HEART

CORE EMOTION:
SHAME

3

4
SECURITY

The Shame Triad

Positioned in the shame triad, type Twos struggle to separate their inherent worth from their perceived worth. The latter is found in what they *do* for others, how they love and serve them. This can lead to pride in their indispensable role and their need to be needed. When trapped in the toxic spiral of shame, Twos believe their worth is wrapped up in what they can give and what they offer to others, which propels them into a never-ending endeavor to earn the love and care they deserve just for being themselves.

Although they are some of the most lovable types on the Enneagram, Twos are prone to let shame keeps them from believing they are indeed loved. *Yeah, but if they really knew . . .* is a phrase shame whispers incessantly. If they really knew your feelings, the ones you're naturally so great at perceiving in others; if they really knew your needs, the ones you instinctively pick up on in those around you; if they *really* knew, then they wouldn't love you. Shame tells the Twos that their worthiness is contingent upon their doing, that their right to belong is based on their service, and that their needs are okay only if they have sufficiently cared for the needs of others first.

The sad part is that within the Christian subculture, where it is more blessed to give than to receive (see Acts 20:35), Twos have been conditioned to give disproportionately, hinging their self-worth on their service. They end up slaving instead of serving, in a frantic endeavor to squelch their shame and earn their enoughness. The underlying narrative, the story they make up, is that "this is my responsibility/job." Thus, they have a difficult time distinguishing the boundary of Christlike service to others versus what they feel they "should" do. *Should* is a major red-flag word for all types but especially Twos. When they cannot bear the load of "shoulds" anymore, we wonder why these otherwise easygoing, kind, and tenderhearted types erupt with fury when their own needs go unattended.

While shame is a struggle for every type and is part of the shared human experience, Twos particularly struggle with the fundamental belief that they are not deserving of love and belonging, that they are not wanted. Much of the work surrounding shame for Twos is rewriting the story they've always told themselves, replacing it with the truth that they are fully wanted and wholly loved.

When stalled out in shame, Twos find themselves propping up their self-image with service because of a fixation on how the world sees them. They reason that if they have pleased others enough, they will be likable and wanted. If they have sufficiently helped and served, then they have earned the right to sit at the table. One of my sorority sisters from college, Christina, is a type Two and is truly delightful to be around. Her warm and calming demeanor and easygoing countenance draws people in, making them feel safe, loved, and wanted. Though we were in the same pledge class and ran in the same circle of friends, I never really *knew* her until our senior year, when we connected over our mutual history of eating disorders and the silence and shame that entails. Christina has an infectious laugh, one that you could hear across the courtyard of our dorms, and she was someone everyone considered their friend. But beneath her polished personality was a girl trapped in the cycle of shame, a girl who believed that she was never quite good enough.

While the belief that she was never enough, or doing enough, led to a relapse in her eating disorder, it also led her to commit to things or help in ways she wasn't gifted in, because she felt like she had to earn her place. Laughing about it now, she recounted agreeing to referee intramural basketball because our sorority needed a few more volunteers. (If you're not familiar with the intensity of college intramurals, think crazy church-league softball but with cussing.) Christina is a beautiful and talented singer—the stage is her field—but organized sports are not something she has much knowledge of or experience in. She volunteered anyway. "I felt like I needed to do it for some reason. Despite the fact that I had zero knowledge to be able to referee, I was assigned an upper level, and the players were furious with me because I had no clue what I was doing!"

We laughed remembering the fleeting hype of intramural games and the memories we shared as sorority sisters, while we mutually ached over the corners shame had pushed us into. We believed that we could earn acceptance and a place at the table by volunteering enough, helping enough, or even losing enough weight.

But that's the trap of shame: enough is never enough. No amount of loving, serving, giving, or attending to will ever be enough to earn what Twos deeply desire: belonging. That is at the core of the Twos' struggle with shame and why they sometimes remain bound by it—they are attempting to earn their way out of shame by meriting the love they long for. But love can never be earned. Love isn't something that can be bought with the relational currency of works.

The Hebrew word *hesed* is used throughout the Old and New Testaments numerous times and loosely translates into English as "love." This translation isn't exact, however, because it speaks more to loyalty and commitment, a faithfulness, steadfastness, and unfailing nature toward the one who is loved. At the crux, *hesed* has nothing to do with us. We are not the initiator or the guarantor. God's covenant with us is not contingent on anything we do.

I can't imagine many things that would cause God's heart to ache more than seeing his children strive and serve to earn something that he has already abundantly given them. For the Two, the invitation is to step out of shame, find freedom from their striving, and rest in the love that has been lavished on them.

Sin Proclivity: Pride

With their radar always alerting them to the feelings and needs of others and playing a supportive role in many of their relationships, pride doesn't seem to fit the Two, but it sneaks up in subtle and unassuming ways. Some Twos may not even resonate with their sin proclivity of pride because they feel that *boastful, self-absorbed*, and *pretentious* are far from accurate characteristics to describe them.

Twos cling to the narrative that their needs and desires are less important, always putting their agenda to the side to meet the needs of others through caretaking and acts of service, all of which can seem noble on the surface. Being uncomfortable in the spotlight and not wanting others to make a fuss over them can be mistaken for humility.

When it comes to their own needs, Twos don't self-forget like type Nines but rather self-abnegate—they reject, renounce, and deny themselves. Rejecting and renouncing their own needs, they sacrifice themselves on the *altar* of service to others. What outwardly looks like service to others can be inappropriate self-sacrifice and abnegation of their own needs. The New Testament is filled with accounts of Jesus, the ultimate picture of service and sacrifice, who did not neglect his physical, personal, or spiritual needs while serving, caring for, or healing others (for example, see Mark 1:35, Luke 5:15–16, and Luke 6:12).

Pride can sneak up on Twos under the guise of "dying to self," which subconsciously takes over as the victimhood mentality: *that was the least they could have done for me since I give so much of myself for them.* But service at the expense of self-sacrifice is actually selfish. Self-abnegation is a form of false humility. When you become self-abnegating in your endeavors to care for others, you unintentionally neglect your soul, which is the source of your love for others.

Safety is the priority of every first responder when they show up to the scene of a 911 call. Ensuring that the scene is secure—no bullets flying, cars speeding by, or potential for exposure to hazardous materials—before they exit the ambulance or helicopter is the priority before they begin to care for the sick or injured. This is ingrained into every firefighter, paramedic, and EMT from their first day on duty. If the scene poses a threat to their safety, they wait to respond until the scene is secure and any threats have been neutralized. This isn't selfish or uncaring to those needing their aid; it is how they ensure they are able to provide care and help to those in need.

When Twos metaphorically fail to ensure scene safety before providing care, they risk serious harm to themselves—even death—which ultimately renders them unable to serve others.

Like first responders, Twos need to be aware of their own needs as they build relationships. While Twos crave connectedness and are wonderful at fostering it, connection can easily become one-sided if Twos are not cognizant. True connection requires vulnerability in allowing others in and humility by asking for help. Frequently Twos don't even realize they have needs and have a hard time seeing *they* need help—until it's too late. "Oh no, I got it" was the phrase Tami, a type Two, often used until it was "too little, too late and my family began to suffer from my snapping." Once the resentment and frustration build up, Twos reach a snapping point, and their pride pits them against others.

Self-sufficiency is another form that pride takes in the type Two. "Striving in my own strength, I think everyone else's needs are up to me to fulfill, and I will either make myself sick trying or be totally down on myself if I feel I can't 'fix it,'" Stacey, a type Two, explained. Boundaries naturally present a challenge to the type Twos because so much of their self-worth is contingent on caring for and serving others. Who would they even be if they had boundaries? How could they possibly say no to others' needs? They tend to take on too many responsibilities, which leads to exhaustion and burnout.

Balancing motherhood, work, and a move, and with another baby on the way, my friend Mandy voiced how she found herself slipping into the sin of pride through self-sufficiency. "As a Two, pride and arrogance can get mixed up, thinking of the two interchangeably," she said. While Twos are far from arrogant, especially Mandy, she went on the say, "I've noticed my thinking lately centers on *me*. I think that I can do it all, that I don't need help, and that is pride."

Although culturally praised, martyrdom isn't something to be celebrated. This martyrdom mindset makes the Two feel that they sacrifice more for others than others would ever be willing to sacrifice for them, and that they could never be loved equal to the way they love others. Twos slip into a presumptuous place of pride when they believe they know exactly what others need and how to best meet those needs. Rather than asking others—or more importantly, God—they swoop in with their own ideas and agendas, believing that the other person needs them, their service, and their solutions. This self-sufficiency mentality robs God of his rightful place as provider and sustainer.

True service empowers others rather than making them dependent on you. When unhealthy and living unaware, Twos give with strings attached, which from a biblical standpoint is neither true service nor true giving. Their generosity comes with unspoken contingencies and the people they care for are left on the hook, unbeknownst to them. Twos operate with IOUs, never cashing them in but always making sure they have enough in circulation in case they ever need them. The scale is never balanced, the playing field is never even, and if it is, they will act swiftly to bring it back to an imbalanced state. This imbalanced state they choose to live in, whether consciously or subconsciously, gives them a sense of security—consolation that their own needs will be taken care of. This can initiate a self-seeking spiral that is not aligned with how love is described in 1 Corinthians 13:4–6. When Twos slip into this spiral, they reduce their love for others to a mere transaction that only serves to make them feel safe.

It can be easy to look condescendingly on any sin proclivity that is not unique to our individual type or that we do not wrestle with so deeply (which ironically is the pride in all our hearts). But when we stop long enough to examine the core desires, the motivations that cause us and our fellow journeymen to stumble into sin, our hearts should overflow with compassion for one another, as Christ's heart does for all of us. For the type Two, their pride is connected to a deep-seated fear that they are not loved for who they are but rather for what they give and how well they care for others, which in turn earns them love and care. The Twos' struggle with pride doesn't equate to them being flawed as a person. It's simply a unique struggle they face, especially since they are positioned in the shame triad.

Virtue and Essence: Humility and Freedom

Embracing their finiteness, Twos find freedom. When they are not under the compulsion to be all things to all people, they allow Christ to be all in all, humbly positioning themselves to be "a vessel for honorable use, set apart as holy, useful to the master of the house, ready for every good work" (2 Timothy 2:21).

As the counterpoint to pride, humility surfaces through true service, which empowers others rather than making them dependent on you. Relinquishing the satisfaction found in playing an indispensable role, Twos are emptied of pride, allowing themselves to be filled with the Holy Spirit and poured out as an offering.

The sacrifice of oneself for another that reflects the way Christ loved the church and gave himself up for her, as stated in Ephesians 5:25, is truly beautiful. That kind of love stems from a place of validation, not from needing to be validated. Knowing they are loved, valued, and wanted is the starting point of wholehearted service for the Two. Serving from an overflow, as an outpouring of the love they have been loved with, is radical and freeing.

Being needed or playing a certain role brings a sense of importance and indispensability because we are rendering something that no one else can. However, this can become a portal to pride. Throughout the New Testament, we find that Jesus didn't heal every sick person he encountered, and he didn't meet every need that was brought to him. Instead, he often withdrew into quiet places for rest and reprieve. He understood the importance of solitude and regularly engaged in it without the fear of it making him less: less needed, less valuable, less God.

Along with the instances in the New Testament where Jesus withdrew in solitude, there were times when he intentionally didn't act. When Mary and Martha sent word to Jesus that their brother Lazarus, whom he loved, was sick, Jesus didn't go to Bethany immediately. He waited two more days, which on the surface may have seemed negligent since he knew Lazarus was going to die. Martha even aired her grief with his decision to wait, saying, "Lord, if you had been here, my brother would not have died" (John 11:21). But even before Lazarus had died, before Jesus made his way to Bethany, he said, "This illness does not lead to death. It is for the glory of God, so that the Son of God may be glorified through it" (John 11:4). It was all done so the greater miracle of resurrecting Lazarus could be accomplished.

There is great humility in recognizing a need but also recognizing what is and is not yours to do. And placing your own needs on the backburner isn't selfless. Honoring your own needs is where the pathway to loving and serving others in humility begins. Selectively saying yes brings freedom. No longer pulled in by pride to compulsively say yes to others' needs, a magnificent freedom awaits the Two—a freedom they in turn can usher the rest of the types into.

My friend Mandy and I entered motherhood eleven days apart from one another. Amid the whirlwind of that crazy change, with brand-new roles and responsibilities, she beautifully balanced engaging meaningfully and letting go appropriately. "Seeing myself as dispensable and replaceable, though not in a self-deprecating way, has been so freeing," she shared one afternoon, as we sat curled up in ink-blue velvet tufted chairs with coffee in hand. "I used to spend my time and energy meeting the needs of people in my outer circle, but then I would be so depleted, I couldn't meet the needs of my inner circle, the people who matter most in my life."

It's easy to chalk up the problem to an issue with balance, feeling like it's a mismatch or misallotment of yeses and noes, but it's hardly that. Motherhood naturally forced a shift in roles and responsibilities for Mandy, and the people who she'd previously served through her job as a fitness coach and as a writer had to shift too. But rather than falling prey to saying yes to everyone and everything, as a spiritually grounded and self-aware type Two, Mandy now invests her time and energy into her indispensable roles first. "Someone else can coach the class at the gym, someone else can write the devotional for the publication, but no one else can be Kyle's wife and no one else can be Luke's mom."

Twos, find freedom by serving in your indispensable roles. People are not going to hate you for saying no. If they do, that's on them and they are obviously not the people in your inner circle. Your people will be understanding, gracious, and proud of you for the growth and work it took for you to say no.

How to Grow as a Type Two

Solitude

Solitude can feel more like a chore than a reprieve for the always working, continually serving Two. They often feel more at peace serving, and anxiety arises when they take a break to get still. It feels downright *wrong* when there is so much to do! But solitude is essential for Twos' growth and transformation. Beginning to incorporate the spiritual practice of solitude into your life doesn't mean you have to stop serving others. It doesn't mean clearing your schedule of all extra activities. Serving is how you display God's love to the world; it is one of your most beautiful spiritual gifts. But solitude can shift your heart and posture you in a position of humility, from which true service flows.

Along with their comrades, types Three and Four, in the

heart-centered triad with the core emotion of shame, solitude is a vital spiritual practice for the type Two. With their default of seeing and making sense of the world through their relationships with others, solitude is imperative for Twos so they can realign and refocus. Profound growth happens when they disconnect from others and reconnect in a meaningful and healthy way with themselves and God.

Solitude quiets the external voices and allows Twos to answer the question, *What is mine to do?* before diving headlong into the list of needs and requests of others. Before Jesus performed miracles, before he healed the sick, he asked what they were seeking. The all-knowing God in the flesh asked what people desired *before* acting. Anticipating needs is great and, Twos, you can see and anticipate better than all other types. But honor those you serve by first asking how you can best love and serve them. By doing so, you honor others while humbly serving them. The way you love people is beautiful and special, but it isn't the benchmark or hallmark way of loving.

Through solitude, the work of transformation that takes place in the heart of the Two is understanding their own value and worth. Because Twos equate their worth and hinge their value on the very roles they play and their responsibilities or service to others, solitude forces them to get away and be present to themselves and God. If you are a Two, reflect on the ways you give of yourself, your time, and your resources to feel worthy, valued, and accepted. Understanding that your identity is in Christ alone is the cornerstone of this transformation—not in what you do or don't do, not in the value you bring or the way you give of yourself, but just in being alive in this world and a dearly loved child of God.

Your identity is in Jesus—not in the people around you, not in the roles you fill. You already belong, just for who you are. You may recognize and know those truths on a cognitive level, but allowing them to embed into your heart is another matter altogether. If you were raised in a way that reinforced your worth being contingent on what you do, or if you received this message from church or organized religion, this process may require deeper work with a trusted therapist. While it may be a simple truth, simple doesn't mean easy. It's not easy to reprogram your head and your heart after years of believing something and functioning within a system and construct that supports it.

Solitude allows the silence and space needed for the Two to truly recognize their motives. This is part of the beauty of the Enneagram and why it can be so helpful in our personal and spiritual growth. Other personality-typing systems (MBTI, DiSC, StrengthsFinder, and so forth) merely speak to behaviors, not the underlying motivations. Twos in an unhealthy place can project an image of being so selfless and so self-giving, all while having the underlying motivation that is centered on receiving. When you engage in solitude, examine your motive for giving. Are you giving from a place of overflow, or are you giving from a place of lack and expect something in return? If it's the latter, realign yourself to the truth that no other person, no role, no job, no child, no experience, no thing can satisfy that need—only Jesus can do that.

Journaling

Understanding motivation is important because we don't always need a behavior overhaul to experience change. Often our behavior itself will not drastically change; it's the motivation for our behavior that has significantly shifted. Journaling is a helpful practice in uncovering motivations. Get still and quiet, and allow your heart to emerge and what is deep within your soul to arise. Examine it and be curious about it. Observe instead of judging; seek understanding instead of tailspinning into shame.

Use these journaling prompts as a jumping-off place to dive deeper into your motives and behaviors:

- What are some fears that arise when you think about saying no? What is something you may need to say no to so you can say yes to yourself and to self-care?
- What are some specific phrases shame whispers to you concerning your worth? Without helping, loving, or serving others, how are you enough?
- Finish the sentence: I need help with _____. Who are two people you can call and ask for help with what you named?

Saying No

When Twos stop serving people from unhealthy and, at times, self-serving motives (validation, love, worth, to receive in return), it is disrupting and upsetting because they are no longer filling the role in the way they always functioned within their systems or constructs (marriage, family of origin, friend group, church, workplace). But this is where you lean into Jesus, finding your peace and satisfaction in him, and where you lean into your core group of people, who will rally around you and encourage you on this journey of growth and transformation.

Start with little noes that don't feel so awful and scary. Saying no is like lifting weights at the gym. If you haven't been in a while, it's going to be hard, and the next day you're going to feel the soreness. But after several weeks you'll find you can lift heavier weights and are conditioned for longer, more strenuous workouts because of the strength and muscle memory you have built. It doesn't mean working out is easy; you are just more conditioned. Saying no will likely never be on your list of easy tasks, but you can condition yourself to be more comfortable with it over time.

Know that it is okay to decommit, which is sometimes necessary for your physical health and for the sake of your soul. Just like saying no, when you back out of a commitment, the world will keep spinning, your people will still love you, God will still love you, and everyone will survive.

On a practical level, you could plan an annual vacation that's far enough away from home that you can't drive back to help out the babysitter or return early to pitch in because someone else bailed. No Internet or phone service is a bonus (I know, that's a hard sell). Let the waitstaff at the resort or restaurant serve you. After all, that is their job and you're paying them for the service—don't feel bad about it.

You can also build some buffer time into your day. Use your daily commute to breathe, pray, clear your mind, and settle yourself before you walk in the door and are bombarded by the needs of kids, dinner that won't cook itself, and endless chores. If you commute down the hall to your home office or are a stay-at-home parent (the actual heroes of the world), bookend your day with a fifteen-minute walk before transitioning into the rest of your schedule.

If you start to feel frustrated and resentment begins to rise up inside, stop and ask yourself, *Am I really okay?* Instead of doing the dishes loudly or dropping not-so-subtle hints that you could use some help, express to your spouse or closest friends that you're feeling unseen, uncared for, and unloved—or maybe that you're just plain tired and could use a little help. Asking for help with the dishes isn't rude or demanding; it's a simple request and a reasonable one at that. It will be uncomfortable and feel confrontational, but like saying no, the phrase "Hey, can you help with _____?" will build muscle memory so you can receive the help you need and deserve without all the clanking dishes and exasperated sighs.

Believe That You Are Wanted

People *want* to love you. Let that sink in for a minute: people *want* to love you. Let others love you. You're worth the meal train and the casserole. You're worth the babysitter so you can have the afternoon off (or just take a nap!), the lunch date, the time to engage in something that feels like self-care. But it will take a shift in mindset to let others love and serve you. You will have to start believing that you are loved and wanted within your inner circle and be open and vulnerable about your wants and needs.

Even with the best intentions, those in your inner circle are going to get it wrong. They're going to misunderstand, they're going to miss the mark, it's going to be clunky and awkward and feel all wrong sometimes. Be quick to let people off the hook you may have placed them on, when the way they love isn't an exact replica of your way. But also let them know explicitly *how* they can best love you. They truly desire to, but it'll take work from both parties to get there. Remember that you're worthy of being loved and cared for and served. You are wanted deeply and desperately for who you are.

REMEMBER

You are wanted.

READ

"But when you give to the needy, do not let your left hand know what your right hand is doing, so that your giving may be in secret. And your Father who sees in secret will reward you." (Matthew 6:3–4)

"For I am sure that neither death nor life, nor angels nor rulers, nor things present nor things to come, nor powers, nor height nor depth, nor anything else in all creation, will be able to separate us from the love of God in Christ Jesus our Lord." (Romans 8:38–39)

"For am I now seeking the approval of man, or of God? Or am I trying to please man? If I were still trying to please man, I would not be a servant of Christ." (Galatians 1:10)

RESPOND

- Don't deprive others of the honor and privilege of caring for you. You don't need to continuously rack up IOUs to cash in when you need it. Others don't see it as owing you—they simply love you and want to care for you.
- When you notice a need, don't reflexively jump to meet it. "Yes" doesn't have to be your default answer. It's a marker of growth when things are asked and demands are placed on you and you can take a breath and say to yourself, *I don't have to meet that need.*
- Check in with yourself. How are you feeling? What do you need? Share your feelings with a trusted friend and schedule a self-care activity that will meet the needs that arise.
- The next time you commit to helping or go to meet a need for someone, stop and ask yourself first, *What is my motivation?* If there's a hint of self-serving or strings attached, reconsider. If it's truly altruistic and you expect nothing in return, go for it!
- Come up with creative ways to love and serve others anonymously.

[8]

TYPE THREE:

HOPE AND AUTHENTICITY

TYPE THREES, ALSO CALLED THE ACHIEVERS or performers, light up the world with the brightest hope, a true testament to the visionaries they are. Type Threes are driven and ambitious, with an energy that others find infectious. They are goal-directed and success-oriented, not only for themselves but also for others, as they champion and support them in accomplishing their dreams.

The essence that type Threes exhibit is authenticity. Authenticity emerges for Threes when they can set aside the masks they instinctively pick up and put on, exposing the beauty of their true selves. When this happens, the tasks they perform and the roles they play to earn love and acceptance fall by the wayside. This is the spiritual journey of the Three.

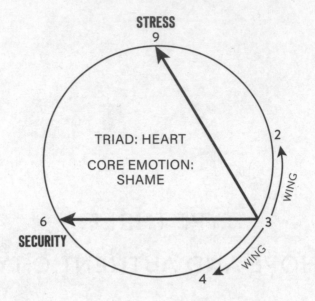

The Shame Triad

Falling into the shame triad (also known as the heart-centered triad, along with type Twos and Fours), the spiritual struggle of the Threes' deceit is often compounded by the shame they continually attempt to evade. We find shame entering the world soon after creation. Adam and Eve were living in sinless perfection until Eve was deceived by the serpent in Genesis 3, which details the fall of man. Upon Eve's deception and Adam following suit, guilt and shame entered the world. Their eyes were indeed opened, as the serpent had promised, and they realized they were naked. So they made clothing out of fig leaves to cover themselves.

Later, in the dialogue between God, Adam, and Eve, God asked, "Who told you that you were naked?" (Genesis 3:11). In the conversation between Eve and the serpent, Eve was never *told* that she and Adam were naked. It was only after they had eaten the fruit of the knowledge of good and evil that their eyes were opened and they were aware of their nakedness. No one told them they were naked—shame told them they were naked. Shame caused them to seek out covering for themselves. That's what shame does: it leads us into hiding, pushing us to cover ourselves and our actions.

The fig leaves can be symbolic for the covering type Threes use. This covering of themselves as a result of shame is not done with fig leaves but rather with the masks they wear and the roles they play to squelch that shame. Yet the tragic irony is that the covering intended to hide shame—the roles and masks—is ultimately deceitful and yields even more shame. This is at the heart of the struggle for the type Three and why the bondage to shame and their sin of deceit is so powerful. They feel shame for their deceit but they deceive because they feel ashamed. What a predicament and despairing place to live. The soul-crushing weight of shame is a death sentence to anyone who finds themselves under its curse.

Deceit is wrong. But whereas wrongdoings are meant to produce guilt in us, for type Threes, toxic shame is often the by-product. Brené Brown defines the difference between shame and guilt in her book *Daring Greatly*: "Shame is 'I am bad.' Guilt is 'I did something bad.'"[1] The shame captured in the Genesis 3 account of the fall encompasses the shame that type Threes bear, the feeling of "I am bad and therefore must cover myself." Type Threes may feel this more profoundly than any other type, which propels them into a life of striving and achieving to outstrip the shame.

"Whether it's actual shame or perceived shame from others, it can send me into a spiral. When I experience shame in a given situation, I will replay it over and over and over until it almost becomes part of my identity," recounted Breehan, a type Three. Shame can color the world Threes live in, bleeding into their work, relationships, and everyday life. It propels them to go more, do more, push more, achieve more, accomplish more, and succeed more in an attempt to silence it.

The shame Threes feel runs so deeply, encoded into the very DNA of their souls, that it is only through the saving work of the gospel that they can ever hope to be freed to live authentically in the fullness of who they were created to be. That's where the profound beauty of type Threes' spiritual journey lies. When they have been freed from their shame and deceit, the very hope they illuminate to the world by living in the authenticity of who they are is the gift they bring.

Sin Proclivity: Deceit

The sin proclivity of the type Three is deceit, which spans from little white lies to entirely fabricated narratives involving themselves and others. Breehan told me about her personal struggle with deceit:

I find myself stretching the truth or flat-out lying often to make myself look better, to make the story more funny, to make my point more dramatic. If I'm in a pickle and feel as though I'm about to get in trouble, I will tell a lie or stretch the truth (which in reality is still a lie) to justify myself or defend my actions. Even in situations where I'm just trying to tell people about myself or making a joke, I struggle with just telling things like they are.

For type Threes, deceit often emerges in projecting a false image of who they are to others. They shape-shift into the type of person, spouse, parent, employee, or friend they think they need to be and therefore can end up in an identity crisis of sorts. Having projected so many images and played so many roles, they can no longer keep straight which role they have played in which setting and what image they have projected to whom. What can be even more imprisoning to type Threes is that the deceit becomes so ingrained they can no longer decipher who they are, aside from the roles they play within the web of deceit they are caught in.

Type Threes can be villainized for this deceit, but understanding where it stems from can foster compassion and understanding from those walking along the journey of spiritual growth with them. What lies beneath Threes' deceit is the belief that who they are is not good enough or worthy of love and that they are worthless aside from what they do. They got lost along the way, sometimes in the attention they received for their performance, equating their worth to what they accomplish and their value in what they bring. Rather than allowing the fundamental and inherent worth they possess as image-bearers of God to be their anchoring point, to feel worthy and valuable, Threes cling to the personas they've created or masks they've put on.

Unfortunately, our culture celebrates their drive and success, masks and all. But this is an enormous disservice to Threes' essence. We esteem their high capacity, productivity, and the results they are capable of producing, only adding more fuel to the fire. In *The Road Back to You* the authors wrote,

> Being a Three and living in America is like being an alcoholic living above a saloon. In our success- and image-obsessed

culture they are more revered and rewarded than any other number on the Enneagram. Is it any wonder spiritual work is hard for them? Because the adaptive strategies of their personality work so well and for so long, they might not start working on themselves spiritually until midlife, or when they fail and can't cover it up.[2]

Deceit, in the form of masks and roles, is what ultimately prevents type Threes from shining forth authentically. But ironically, these masks and roles are the very things that have gotten them to where they are. They are survival tactics as well as social personas that have led to "success." Threes become so buried underneath the masks and roles that who they are is smothered, leaving only shadows and a mere shell of a human being. That is why it is so hard for Threes to do the work of spiritual transformation, setting aside the deceit and walking into the light of authenticity: they are admired and appreciated for those roles.

Perhaps the greatest deceit they live with is that they *are* in fact the masks they wear and the roles they play. This belief is often subconscious, one that is so deeply rooted it has infiltrated every part of their existence. Many cannot remember a time, even back to early childhood, when they were not performing or playing a role to gain others' applause and adoration. This is why the subconscious belief that they are their roles and masks prevails.

Many type Threes do not realize the breadth and depth of this deception until they experience the stereotypical midlife crisis or undergo a personal or professional failure they cannot conceal, leaving them exposed. Often that is when this deception shifts from their subconscious into consciousness, and they are forced to confront the truth of who they are against the roles they have spent their entire lives playing. They have become so familiar with their masks that they no longer know what the face underneath looks like. This is hard and painful work for the type Three. It is so vast and overwhelming that when it surfaces, it is far easier to box it up and put it on the shelf, with half-hearted intentions of dealing with it later. Or they medicate themselves with work, success, alcohol, sex, experiences, substances—anything to take the edge off the pain.

We all have borne witness, maybe from afar or closer in proximity than we wished, as the quintessential type Three American pastor has fallen fast and hard from his esteemed, regarded, and respected position into an affair, addiction, or some other sort of deception. When I witnessed this firsthand within a church I attended, it was startling, shocking, and devastating. I saw someone I had deep respect for, who had been formative in my own faith, fall so far. But perhaps the most disheartening part was watching this man struggle, after everything had been found out and brought to light, to be truthful with himself and others. The deception had run so deep for so long that it must have felt impossible for him to reconcile the masks he'd worn and the man underneath.

Sadly, for many type Threes, a personal or professional failure of tremendous magnitude is the catalyst for bringing that unconscious deceit to their awareness for the first time. The deceit Threes struggle with can be as complex as the images they project and roles they play or as simple as cutting corners, only telling the parts of the story that benefit them, or telling dumb lies. Regardless of the simplicity or complexity, for the spiritually disconnected and distant Three, the subconsciousness of the deceit persists. Bringing consciousness to this deceit is where the pathway home to reconnection with themselves and God begins.

Virtue and Essence: Hope and Authenticity

For type Threes who have done the work to bring deceit from their subconscious into consciousness—stripping themselves of their projected personas so that they are no longer enslaved to their shame-driven performances—they are able to shine forth the virtue of the brightest hope. If it's possible for the type Three to find freedom from the enslavement of their shame through the atoning work of Christ on the cross, then there is hope for us all.

This is where the essence of type Threes emerges. As the masks and roles are set aside, as they step off their performance stage, they are able to step into authenticity. No longer a cheap impersonation, they become real. In the book *The Velveteen Rabbit*, Margery Williams wrote in a lovely and childlike way, through a conversation between the Skin Horse and the Velveteen Rabbit, about what it means to become real:

> "Real isn't how you are made," said the Skin Horse. "It's a thing that happens to you. When a child loves you for a long, long time, not just to play with, but REALLY loves you, then you become Real."
>
> "Does it hurt?" asked the Rabbit.
>
> "Sometimes," said the Skin Horse, for he was always truthful. "When you are Real you don't mind being hurt."
>
> "Does it happen all at once, like being wound up," he asked, "or bit by bit?"
>
> "It doesn't happen all at once," said the Skin Horse. "You become. It takes a long time. That's why it doesn't often happen to people who break easily, or have sharp edges, or who have to be carefully kept. Generally, by the time you are Real,

most of your hair has been loved off, and your eyes drop out and you get loose in the joints and very shabby. But these things don't matter at all, because once you are Real you can't be ugly, except to people who don't understand."[3]

For type Threes, understanding first and foremost that they are loved by God—for *who* they are, exactly as they were created, not for the roles they fill or their perfect performance—and then by others is the cornerstone of their authenticity. Sometimes this process does hurt. There are hard moments of failure. There are painful moments of exposure, confronting who actually lies beneath those masks and roles. There's something deep and leveling, on both a soul and gut level, in realizing that you've been living falsely, acknowledging that you've been lying to yourself and others by walking the hard and humble path of repentance toward restoration.

Authenticity, becoming real, doesn't happen all at once, just as the Skin Horse explained to the Velveteen Rabbit. It's a process, a journey taken one step at a time, one day at a time. Authenticity doesn't require a cleaned-up version of yourself or a completed to-do list. It does, however, require you to dismantle the lies upon which you've built your identity:

that you don't have much to offer outside of your work,
that who you are is what you do, or
that you have to earn your right to belong and be loved.

But authenticity is never ugly. Authenticity is *who* and *how* you were created, an image-bearer of Christ, illuminating hope to the rest of the world.

How to Grow as a Type Three

Solitude

Type Threes spend their days looking at themselves through the lens of others, scrutinizing their work performance through the eyes of their boss, rehashing a conversation from the perspective of their spouse, thinking about how they will look to the friend or colleague they are meeting with this afternoon. They make sense of their world through the context of their relationships, from the desires, emotions, and reactions of others. Solitude grounds Threes by pulling them out of this constant feedback loop and into a place of quietness within themselves and before the Lord.

Solitude is not synonymous with loneliness. While both words connote being alone, loneliness is a state of disconnection, while solitude is a sacred space of deep connection. Until type Threes begin a regular and intentional practice of solitude, they may not realize how disconnected they are from themselves and from God. This state of disconnection compounds shame and further drives them to pick up their masks and step into the roles they are accustomed to playing. Engaging in a practice of solitude helps type Threes step off the performance stage and see themselves only through the eyes of their Creator, so their authenticity can emerge.

All the spiritual practices—silence, solitude, and stillness—are best practiced when we can find time and space away from the hurried rhythms of life and the noise of our feeds, phones, and daily lives. For the types in the heart triad (Two, Three, and Four), whose core emotion is shame, it is important that this practice be engaged in when they are physically alone.

Viewing themselves in relationship to God, not in relationship to others, grants Threes the eternal perspective that will propel them on their journey of transformation. They will always feel the pull to kick it up a notch, hit another income goal, and do more, but an eternal perspective for the Three comes in the simplicity of everyday life. It's gained in spending time with Jesus, conversations with your spouse or friends, playing with your kids—those are the things that are of eternal significance and value: God, his Word, and people.

"Distraction reigns when I'm trying to practice solitude," Alex, a type Three, shared. Threes need to intentionally carve out time in their schedules for spiritual practices and set a rhythm that will guide them in spiritual disciplines. Otherwise, this will fall lower and lower on the to-do list, until it eventually is neglected for the sake of more work, accomplishments, or success. 1 Timothy 4:7–8 can remind Threes of this priority: "Rather train yourself for godliness; for while bodily training is of some value, godliness is of value in every way, as it holds promise for the present life and also for the life to come."

Physical training in the realm of work, accomplishments, and success is of some value; no one would argue that it isn't. But training in godliness is of eternal value. Threes, focus on prioritizing that. Turn off your phone when you go to bed at night. When you wake up, leave it on the charger. Don't reach for it until it's time to start work for the day. Take time to wake up, drink coffee, read, write, and pray, setting the tone for the day. It's harder to *find* time in your day than it is to *take* the time you need first thing in the morning.

Helpful Rhythms

A practice for Threes that may feel extremely unproductive is breathing. Along with many physiological benefits, such as increasing oxygen consumption, purposeful breathing brings a physical rhythm and cadence that helps to ground you. Set a timer for five minutes. Inhale as you count to five, hold your breath at the peak of your inhale for a count of five, and exhale as you count to five. If you have an Apple Watch, it has a setting that will alert you hourly to breathe. Just don't dismiss it each hour when it buzzes to remind you.

Meditation, though important for any type, is particularly helpful for Threes, to tune out others' voices, thoughts, and opinions by focusing on the present moment, alone with themselves. In the "Read" section at the end of this chapter, I've included some Bible verses that may be especially impactful for type Threes to meditate on.

Outdoor walks under the expanse of the sky and surrounding world, whether it's a quiet nature trail or a bustling city street, are a great way for type Threes to find aloneness with themselves and God. To combat the frantic feeling of "doing nothing," moving your body while quieting your mind allows you to be attuned to the voice of God, which often speaks in still, small moments. Filter your thoughts—especially those that involve God and what he wants from you or how he sees you—carefully. If they are intense in nature, with a feeling of duty, obligation, or "I need to do XYZ," they are likely a projection of how you view yourself rather than what God wants from you.

Journaling

Journaling for a few minutes daily about their thoughts and feelings can help Threes connect with the hearts that they often live disconnected from. This can be perplexing since type Threes are in the heart-centered triad. They are aware of the emotions of others but often unaware of their own. Like type Fives, sometimes Threes must think their way into their feelings, connecting that pathway from their head to their heart. The practice of journaling can be beneficial in this way and even allow Threes to explore more creative activities, such as writing poetry or short stories, which they may normally view as unproductive.

To practice connecting with your heart through your feelings, use the journal prompts below as a guide:

- Can you differentiate shame and guilt in your life? What does shame feel like? What does guilt feel like?
- Is there something you regularly use to medicate the pain of shame? Some examples could be work, alcohol or other substances, sex, experiences, relationships, or activities like watching TV or scrolling through social media.
- Finish the sentence: If I could internalize the truth that I am loved for who I am and not my accomplishments, I would _____.

Stepping off the Stage

It's imperative for Threes to have a few people who know *everything* about them. A spouse may be one person, but having a mentor or a few close friends they regularly check in with will be vital to walking in truth and authenticity. When these people ask, "How are you doing?" they don't want to hear about your work—they want to hear about your heart. They're safe people to confess your failures to and share your fears.

Living in the light of community conditions Threes in humility, which is the companion they will need for their journey of transformation. As a sort of powerhouse type, it can be easy for them to slip into pride, but when humility is their default setting, the focus is no longer on them: it shifts to God and others. It's hard to continue down a pathway of deceit when your focus is on loving God and loving others. And remember, everyone else is wildly insecure as well. Just be humble and real, and people will love you for *you*.

For those who are in close relationships with type Threes, find practical ways you can help them create margin to engage in solitude. If it's your spouse or a friend, offer to watch the kids for an hour so they can escape to a place of solitude. If it's an employee or colleague, encourage them to slip out of the office thirty minutes earlier to utilize that time to engage in a solitude practice. They're probably staying late anyway because that's what type Threes do. Verbally affirm them for their character and *who* they are rather than what they have done or accomplished. Their authenticity invites you to step into your own, living fully and truly as you were created. What a gift Threes are to the world.

Seeing a spiritually evolved Three who has stepped off the performance stage and embraced the authenticity of who they are is a living, breathing testament to the work of the gospel in the hearts of men. The hope they shine forth brightens the darkness of the world and casts a vision for the other eight types of the freedom found in living authentically.

REMEMBER

You are loved simply for who you are.

READ

"Come to me, all who labor and are heavy laden, and I will give you rest. Take my yoke upon you, and learn from me, for I am gentle and lowly in heart, and you will find rest for your souls. For my yoke is easy, and my burden is light." (Matthew 11:28–30)

"Turn my eyes from looking at worthless things;
 and give me life in your ways." (Psalm 119:37)

"It is in vain that you rise up early and go late to rest,
 eating the bread of anxious toil;
 for he gives to his beloved sleep." (Psalm 127:2)

RESPOND

- Go to bed a half hour earlier and wake up a half hour earlier to engage in a solitude practice. (Work can wait—it really can).
- Get outside and go for a walk by yourself. Bundle up if it's cold; succumb to the sweat if it's sweltering.
- When you're sitting at stoplights while driving, practice breathing in for five seconds, holding for five seconds, and breathing out for five seconds.
- Keep a journal and spend even just five minutes per day writing down your thoughts, feelings, or what you're grateful for.
- Once a week, go to coffee with or call someone with whom you can practice being your authentic self. This list may be very small at first, but begin to expand it. Try not to repeat someone for at least a month.

9

TYPE FOUR:
ORIGIN AND EQUANIMITY

TYPE FOURS, THE INDIVIDUALISTS OR ROMANTICS, are original and introspective and embody authenticity, distinguishing themselves from the other eight types. Finely attuned, Fours are keen when it comes to emotions, both their own and others'. Being able to bear witness to pain without needing to run from it, attempt to fix it, or offer sweet nothings to medicate it, their ability to empathize is rare.

The evenness of mind found in the essence of equanimity for the Four tempers the elated and depressed states that otherwise seek to steal their contentedness in life. When Fours stand firmly in the sureness and completeness of the atoning work of the cross, they find peace with their imperfections instead of being sucked into the shame spiral. Rather than being enslaved to envy, spiritually awakened Fours are grounded in gratitude, which brings balance and steadfastness.

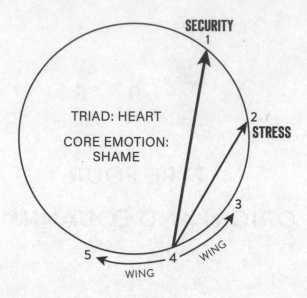

The Shame Triad

Rounding out the shame triad, Fours feel as though something within them is missing and incomplete, that they are fundamentally flawed. Their unique and individualistic nature can compound this belief at times since they think others don't "get" them.

While shame is an emotion common to the human experience, regardless of Enneagram type, Fours' shame can turn toxic, leading them to feel ostracized instead of different, isolated rather than individualistic. Shame can become all-encompassing and pervasive. Jess, a type Four, recounted the first time she remembered realizing shame was what she was experiencing: "I thought, *Oh, if this is shame, everything about my life is shame. I am swimming in shame or stuck in a shame spiral constantly.* It felt like I *am* shame."

Lily, another type Four shared, "Getting onto the bus in third grade, I walked down the aisle toward the row I sat on every day with the same two girls. When I got to the row to take my usual seat, they said, 'You don't fit here anymore.' In that moment, I remember thinking to myself, *The verdict is in: I'm fat, I don't fit, I don't belong.*"

This heartbreaking encounter shrouded Lily in shame as she journeyed into middle and high school. "There were specific standards, and it was clearly communicated to me how I *could* look, how I *should* look. My mom and I used to go to classes at the YMCA and I distinctly remember this one girl, we were the same height, but she was 110 pounds. My mom would always make a comment about her, how that's what we could look like. It was all spoken so casually but there is nothing casual about shame," she shared.

While body image shame is not unique to type Fours, shame is suffocating for them because they cannot see a shameful experience separate from *who* they are. With shame engulfing their bodies and occupying enormous brain space, Fours struggle to stay present because there is little to no margin left in their minds. They get stalled out and stuck in shame. The pervasiveness of shame is what makes it so dangerous and debilitating. Shedding the shame that shrouds Fours, whether shame from their own sin or shame from others and experiences, ultimately requires the blood of Christ, the reversal agent for the curse.

Hiding in their shame, Fours endorse the idea that something is fundamentally flawed in them, that something is missing. When they adopt a "people don't understand me" mindset, this can become an easy way to keep others out, holding them at arm's length. Unaware Fours can find themselves in an endless game of cat and mouse, continually wanting to be pursued by others and drawn out but dashing away the moment they are seen. Intentionally making themselves elusive, they reason that people "won't get them anyway." This ideology is isolating, which is exactly how shame thrives. Turning a painful, albeit normal, human emotion into something toxic, Fours believe that they are hopelessly broken, that they *are* shameful.

"For most of my life I've struggled to understand my feelings consciously. I knew they were there and were powerful, but they sort of *were* me rather than being something that happened within me or an experience," said Mara, a type Four. Because shame is their core emotion, that's why it's so tricky and can slip into a toxic space. Part of the journey of freedom and wholeness for the type Four is in seeing the emotions as experiences rather than synonymous with themselves. Mara went on to share, "I'm starting to be able to see my feelings as separate from me, to watch and notice them but be able to choose what to do about them."

After hijacking our higher mind to make us feel fundamentally flawed and stealing our sense of being known, the last place shame wants us to find ourselves is at the foot of the cross. Because there we find fellow sinners and sufferers all plagued by the shared experience of shame. At the foot of the cross, the playing field is level for everyone who has ever knelt there. The isolation shame thrives in is rendered powerless over those who come to Calvary.

That is the great invitation to all, but especially to the type Four. The invitation in the outstretched arms of the crucified Christ is into communion with him and community with others. Christ is the only one who can *fully* see, know, and understand you. But there are people, if given the opportunity through empathy, who will see, know, and accept you. Understanding isn't a prerequisite to acceptance.

Being known can feel scary, and the filter of shame can magnify that fear. The question Fours will have to honestly answer is, *Am I allowing other people in?* Making assumptions that people won't understand or "get" them isn't a justifiable reason to keep others at bay and to remain elusive. Being known requires that you reveal yourself, and being found means you must stop running. Freedom from toxic shame is found in togetherness.

Sin Proclivity: Envy

On a foundational level, Fours feel as though something is missing, that something is wrong with them. The feeling of incompleteness is so visceral that trying to convince them otherwise is futile. Believing they are tragically flawed, Fours can be hijacked by envy before they even know it.

Envy and comparison are close companions, and what starts out as seemingly small comparisons can grow into untamed envy. A strange duality is at play with Fours and envy. They long to be unique, yet they compare themselves to others, thinking that acquiring what everyone else has, attaining what they have achieved, will connect them more to the world and others. Envy arises when, instead of channeling their energy into the beauty of creative differences between them and others, they look longingly at what others have that they don't, believing that attaining or achieving that will bring them fulfillment and completeness.

Longing for what is whole and right, true and good, perfect and complete will always live deep in our souls. Longing is what reminds us that this earth is not our home, that we were created for more, that Jesus is the only thing that will satisfy us, complete us, and make us whole. But when our eyes are no longer fixed on Jesus, we begin noticing what others have that we lack. When a brief glance turns into a long look, we begin to fixate, our desire rises to an inordinate level, and we can slip into covetousness. Covetousness was considered such a serious sin with far-reaching effects that in Exodus, it was specifically addressed in the tenth and final commandment (see Exodus 20:17).

Covetousness is a self-centered waste of time that hinders and harms our souls. At best, envy is laziness if it is something within your realm of control (yourself and your actions, because those are the only things you have control over) that you are refusing to act on. At worst, envy is a defiant act of unbelief in the sovereignty of God, when it pertains to things you cannot control or change (everyone and everything else in the world), and a lack of gratitude for what God has given and allowed in the story he is writing for you.

The enemy uses envy to get us to question God's goodness and rob us of our hard-won peace. A type Four, Amanda, illustrated this beautifully when she told of transitioning into motherhood after welcoming her first child. She had an opportunity to pitch the book idea that she had been dreaming of writing and working toward for a few years. She knew it wasn't the right time; her anxiety spiked every time she thought about it, and she felt scattered and still not herself after having a baby. She couldn't stand the thought of passing up the opportunity but over the years has learned the gift of waiting and the reward for obedience. "It's not 'now or never,'" she reminded herself, "it's just 'later.'"

A few months later, when the announcement was made

congratulating the newest authors of the publishing houses, she immediately felt frustrated, disappointed, and then envious, thinking, *Why couldn't I have been the one to get the publishing deal?*

The peace she'd felt in passing on the opportunity, as hard as it had been at the time, was hijacked by jealousy in an instant. "I had a decision to make in that moment," she explained. "I could either trust God with the decision I had made in faith or allow distrust to evolve into envy and rob me of peace and joy."

Longing and desire, like emotions, are not good or bad, right or wrong. They are a neutral part of the human experience. When we fail to keep our eyes on the Author and Perfector of our faith and aren't mindful, what we crave turns into coveting and the thoughts we entertain can easily become what we envy. Envy is poison to the soul because gratitude can no longer grow, and contentedness can't be cultivated in envy's presence.

Virtue and Essence: Origin and Equanimity

The spiritual journey of the Four is back to where they were derived from and begotten, to their original source and creator, God. The essence of the Fours, how they reflect Christ to the world, is found through equanimity, or balance. When spiritually anchored, Fours can mirror the many characteristics and varied attributes of a multifaceted God, one who remains constant throughout time and space.

The facets of God make up his complete character; the parts of who he is are unchanging. His justice and mercy, righteousness and goodness, omniscience and omnipotence, graciousness and lovingkindness, holiness and wisdom. That's who he *is*. The fact that even God's emotions change should be a clue that feelings are not final. For instance, the Israelites knew all too well of God's changing emotions toward them. More than once in Exodus, God's anger burned hot against the Israelites because of their rebellion and faithlessness, so much so that he wanted to consume and destroy them. But he relented from harming them, showing mercy from his deeply compassionate heart. His character remained the same and the facets of who he is did not change, but his feelings did.

Feelings are often the guiding force for the Four. They contain a powerful pull that is important to pay attention to. But like a compass, they are merely a guide. They are not always facts, coordinates leading to a precise location. Feelings are information—they are not *who* you are. And yet it is important for Fours to know and rely on the indicators their emotions bring when they are surrendered to God. Jess, the Four who battled shame growing up, explained,

> I've learned over the years, when it comes to my emotions, that when I am grounding myself in biblical truth, fixing my eyes on Jesus, seeking wisdom and guidance in submission to the Lord, I *can* trust my emotions as a guide and pay attention to how they are prompting me and what they are trying to tell me.

The Fours' essence of equanimity comes when they are rooted in Christ, in the finished work of salvation that has made them whole and complete, fundamentally not lacking anything. From this vantage point, Fours can observe their feelings and learn from them without being consumed by them. This is where balance emerges—balance with the truth of the gospel and emotional health for the Four. After finding this new dimension, where they are engaged but not engulfed, informed but not acting impulsively, their emotions become powerful propellants on their spiritual journey.

As Fours learn to engage their emotions in a trusting and balanced manner, they will come to recognize emotions that can be helpful or harmful. With emotions like shame and guilt, there is a duality at play. Guilt, which can produce good fruit in our lives through repentance, can evolve into toxic shame when we internalize the belief that *we are* bad and shameful rather than the belief that what *we did* was bad. Whether it's guilt that can bring good or shame that has turned toxic, both require a sacrifice, a covering, for freedom and atonement. When the shame spiral sucks you in, the Holy Spirit is your only hope of being pulled to safety. When the guilt is too overwhelming to lift your eyes up, the love of God is greater still.

In the Christian world, we often focus primarily on the problem of sin and Jesus' death on the cross that atoned for our sins. While these elements of the story are vital components of the narrative, they don't complete it. Fours, when you hear only that part of the narrative—the sin and sacrifice—and when you live only those aspects of the story, you are missing the origin and perfection of Eden, how the world was initially created.

In the garden, man and God dwelt together in goodness and glory. That was the beginning of the story. The Bible starts in Genesis 1 with the creation of a sinless, spotless, perfect world— not chapter 3, where Eve and the serpent cross paths and sin enters the equation. All too often, we live our lives starting in chapter 3 and we forget the original goodness and glory. Yes, sin entered the world and Christ had to come and die to make atonement for our sins. But the other part of the story is that he ascended back into glory. Instead of fixating on the original sin, focus on the original glory and turn your gaze toward eternal glory. We began in glory, and we will end in glory. That's how the story begins and ends: from glory to glory. Of course, there's also the middle part, which we live in now. It is often painfully, disastrously, all but hopelessly broken and dark. Shame arises because we live in the shadowy spaces of sin and suffering. Though we remain in a sin-filled world with sinful tendencies, until we enter our eternal glory, that is not your identity. Shame doesn't define you; it's Christ in you, the hope of glory, which *is* your identity.

How to Grow as a Type Four

Solitude

When Fours engage in the spiritual practice of solitude, which is a cardinal practice for the shame/heart triad, they are able to confront their authentic selves apart from their emotions. Initially this will be frightening for type Fours, as many cannot imagine who they are aside from their feelings. Because of the powerful pull of their emotions, Fours often believe they *are* their emotions. That is why solitude is the antidote. The spiritual practice keeps them grounded in the present, in touch with the reality of who God is and who they are in him, instead of perpetually on the rollercoaster of agony and ecstasy in their emotions.

Voluntarily electing to withdraw for a period of time in solitude helps Fours buffer themselves from being bombarded by the emotions often elicited in relationships. Life is full of experiences—happy, sad, high, and low—but you don't have to live the experience.

It can be something happening *around* you, not *to* you. Being in solitude with themselves and God is where Fours can find their footing. Solitude brings balance to their emotions so that type Fours can embrace the equanimity that allows them to shine brightest.

During your time of solitude, these journal prompts may help you navigate your emotions and organize your thoughts:

- Personify your emotions by creating characters out of them and write about your interactions with them. What do you notice when you interact with your emotions rather than *feeling* them?
- Instead of slipping into nostalgia over the past, what does embracing the present moment look like practically, even if it's not all you had hoped for?
- In what ways are you uniquely distinct from others? Conversely, how are you inextricably connected to other human beings around you, through your similarities?

Connect with Your Body

Fours, rather than retreating to spend time in and with your feelings, mindful meditation can be a powerful practice to help engage your minds and bodies. As a Four, emotions will never be far from you, but you can spend time assessing them, looking at them, and thinking about them rather than *feeling* them. Separate your feelings from your thoughts—they are not one and the same—and find what your body may be trying to tell you. Begin to see your emotions as an ebb and flow throughout the river of your life. Observe how they connect with other things rather than keeping them as the central focus with crashing, tumultuous currents; they can instead be a small, serene brook.

When the past beckons you, acknowledge it and allow it to pass by. Appropriately assess and learn from it, but leave it there in the past and look ahead toward the future. This requires realism from the Four, accepting what is here and now, not what was or what could have been.

Connecting with your body, understanding its physical limits as well as the strength you possess, will foster that connection. Go on a strenuous hike or try out a fitness class (for example, barre, hot yoga, cycling, or CrossFit). Literally ground yourself in the present moment, with your bare feet in the grass or the sand, or sit on an overlook. With physical exercise, the added benefit of an endorphin release (neurotransmitters in your brain that act on your opiate receptors to diminish pain—think "feel-good" hormones) can be especially helpful for Fours to experience significant mood shifts. Engaging their body instead of defaulting to their emotions also can help Fours develop a healthy realism.

Look for Beauty

As a Four, you see all that is wrong and terrible—you can't help but see it. But when you immerse yourself in the news and world events, you can't think about anything else. Everything becomes ugly, and you can't see the beauty. Therefore, I encourage you to seek out what is beautiful, whether mundane or magnificent. For instance, you could watch the sunset three times a week.

However, if you can't see anything beautiful around you, go create something. Many Fours are naturally drawn to creative careers because this allows them to infuse beauty into the world. Photograph a moment in time the way you saw it, the beauty you experienced in it. Paint something with bold and bright colors, bake something delicious to eat, arrange colorful blossoms in a vase, or write something with soul. Create in a way that showcases the unique beauty you see, which will help you remember that it's there and give others the gift of seeing it through your eyes.

Make Peace with the Tension Between Beauty and Pain

Remember that the energy and emotion that is spent in longing for what was or what could be is better spent channeled into attainable goals with daily commitments that will get you there. This is where Fours will have to reckon with the mundane nature of tasks that will ultimately propel them forward. This is so much of the Christian life. It's made up of ordinary days rather than mountaintop moments; it's daily decisions that culminate over a lifetime. Fours will have to realize that sometimes their situation or circumstance is not special but rather part of a shared human experience and part of the journey of faith, which is beautiful in its own ordinary way.

The ability of Fours to hold the tension of living in a world filled with extraordinary beauty and excruciating pain is a distinct and unique gift. They can balance the light and dark, hurt and hope, sadness and gladness. Living with gratitude for the gift of life and longing for more at the same time beckons the rest of us to do the same. The redeemed Four may know more richly and deeply the truth and beauty of the words Frederick Buechner penned in his novel *Godric*: "What's lost is nothing to what's found, and all the death that ever was, set next to life, would scarcely fill a cup."[1]

This world is indeed filled with bewildering darkness and devastating pain. But God's goodness continually pursues us and will not stop until we are restored at last to our original state of glory, only more beautiful because we have been redeemed.

REMEMBER

You are seen, loved, and beautiful just as you are.

READ

"There is therefore now no condemnation for those who are in Christ Jesus. For the law of the Spirit of life has set you free in Christ Jesus from the law of sin and death." (Romans 8:1–2)

"Now I rejoice in my sufferings for your sake, and in my flesh I am filling up what is lacking in Christ's afflictions for the sake of his body, that is, the church, of which I became a minister according to the stewardship from God that was given to me for you, to make the word of God fully known, the mystery hidden for ages and generations but now revealed to his saints. To them God chose to make known how great among the Gentiles are the riches of the glory of this mystery, which is Christ in you, the hope of glory." (Colossians 1:24–27)

"But you, LORD, are a shield around me,
  my glory, the One who lifts my head high.
  I call out to the LORD,
  and he answers me from his holy mountain."
                (Psalm 3:3–4 NIV)

RESPOND

- Focus on what has been found. There will always be something that's lost, missing, tragic, and flawed, but be intentional about making what's found the focal point.
- You will always see the suffering and feel what is flawed on a deeper level than most, but be quick to focus your efforts on what you can do about the suffering and on fixing what is flawed.
- When you feel yourself being drawn into the past, pull yourself into the present by being grateful for what is here, now. Not what was, what could have been, or what could be in the future. There's a reason there are so many clichés about the present being a gift; it's true.
- Avoid allowing your mood to dictate your decisions. Start small and follow through, keeping commitments even when you don't feel like it.
- Cultivate empathy for others and yourself by seeing how you are similar instead of how you are different. Being similar doesn't mean your element of specialness is lost.

10

TYPE FIVE:

TRANSPARENCY AND

OPENHANDEDNESS

THE INVESTIGATORS, TYPE FIVES, SEE AND
hear everything. They are constantly taking in information and
bring incredible perspective and neutrality to situations. They are
bright and brilliant beings, steady and with an even, calming presence. Inventive and inquisitive, Fives ask open-ended questions,
which allows them to be more objective. They make decisions
based on knowledge instead of emotion and remain unbiased
even when this is uncomfortable for others. If there's a cardinal
saying for Fives, it's "Give me some time to think about it."

The virtue of the type Five is transparency, and their essence
is found in openhandedness. When they can appropriately detach
from their allotted energy and resources, they are able to receive
abundantly more than they could ask or imagine from Christ

(Ephesians 3:20). The spiritual work for the Five lies in opening their hands instead of clenching their fists in fear of being without. The beauty in this work is that opening their hands in sacrifice leaves their palms up, positioning them to receive the sufficiency of Christ.

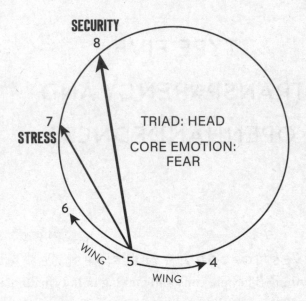

SECURITY
8

7
STRESS

TRIAD: HEAD

CORE EMOTION:
FEAR

6

WING   5 ————▸ 4
WING

The Fear Triad

Fives have a complicated relationship with their emotions. Often they must think their way into their feelings, which makes it fitting that they are part of the head triad. Although they may seem aloof at times, Fives simply live in the cerebral sphere, and this behavior isn't meant as an affront. Fortified by the knowledge and information they have accumulated, Fives position themselves against any invasion by people, processes, or problems that could cause them to be perceived as ignorant, incompetent, or useless.

Fives are better able to access the recesses of their heart and the depths of their soul when they're alone, as they prefer to be, which enables them to feel. Feelings can be fragile territory for Fives; the unknown and uncertainty are both uncomfortable. Because they fear being ignorant, incompetent, and useless, it is important for type Fives to be heard and not dismissed when they offer their thoughts and insight, especially when they share their emotions.

The energy required for Fives to voluntarily offer their insight and advice is considerable since they constantly combat the feeling of never knowing quite enough. It requires even more energy for them to feel their emotions and express them because they reason that their energy would be better spent in the recesses of their mind, pondering, thinking, and problem-solving. They will withdraw from situations or conversations that have the potential to spark emotions. To avoid situations that may cause them to feel incompetent or ignorant, Fives fortify themselves with knowledge, staying in their heads rather than making the eighteen-inch trek down to their hearts, where they may have to vulnerably say, "I don't know." When it comes to emotions, they tell themselves, *Just don't think about that*, so they subsequently will not have to feel them.

Although they share the core emotion of fear with type Sixes and type Sevens, you will be hard-pressed to meet a Five whose fear reverberates in the way that sometimes accompanies the anxiety of a Six or the frenzied energy of a Seven, who is stuck. While the core emotion is the same, Fives have a way of quieting and quelling that fear, seeking to gain mastery over it with the thoughts of their mind. Since fear is an emotion and emotions may take up too much bandwidth, Fives find themselves attempting to avoid fear by withdrawing and carefully protecting their inner resources.

Fives fear being left utterly depleted, emptied of all their energy, and stripped of their resources. It may seem silly and like an extreme, exaggerated response, but this is why Fives will suddenly disappear from social settings. "When we have people over for dinner or host parties, I will reach my limit of social interaction about halfway through and retreat to my bedroom," Jim, a type Five, said. Sharing a similar sentiment, Aubrey stated, "I just cannot hang. Every time we go somewhere, I will socialize for a little bit and then I'm just done for the night." But because they have a strong sense of commitment to obligation, Fives aren't the type to ghost. They will simply and straightforwardly tell you that they will see you later and then physically, mentally, and emotionally retreat.

Fives are not antisocial; they're quite the opposite. They may not seem enthusiastic when asked how they're feeling, because they'll pause and ponder before responding. Yet they are compelling and stimulating to converse with when they give you their time, attention, and energy. But they have a limited reserve of energy and when it's gone, it's gone. They cannot shotgun a Red Bull like their fellow head-triad comrades, the Sevens, and rally for another social outing or stay up half the night. They would need a year to recover from such a thing. But they do often have more energy than they think they do.

Like types Six and Seven, Fives can easily fall into a scarcity mindset, believing they will not have enough. This fear feeds into their relational and emotional detachment, propelling them into a place of further withdrawal and isolation when left unchecked. A large portion of type Fives' bandwidth is taken up by people—trying to read them and their emotions. Fearing that being connected to others will drain them dry, Fives limit not only their social interactions but the connectedness they allow themselves to experience even with those closest to them. Believing that their needs are a problem, Fives withdraw and disconnect further because this mindset of scarcity has caused them to conclude that they must be the ones to meet their own needs.

Jim, who had worked in higher education most of his career, had an office with an outer room that housed dozens of books and was separated by a door from an inner office, where he would work from his desk. Reflecting back, he perceived that office as a curious metaphor for the Five: an office within an office, the outer one containing knowledge and the inner one where he actually sat.

As is often the preference of a type Five, the separation of the two offices made him less accessible than the professors who occupied the surrounding offices. But true growth for the type Five happens when they learn how to let people into that inner office, opening themselves up to receiving love and support. That is the purpose and function of the body of Christ. As humans, we are incapable of true self-sufficiency and were never meant to be siloed. We shrivel when deprived of contact, conversation, and communion with people; relationships are our lifeblood. The body of Christ, made up of many members all serving different functions, is a source of support. The work for the Five entails seeing and embracing the body as a source of Christ's sufficiency—*his* body, full of people who are ready, willing, and wanting to love, serve, and care for them.

Sin Proclivity: Avarice

When it comes to their time, energy, and resources, Fives fear insufficiency, which can run rampantly as their sin proclivity of avarice—an excessive or inordinate desire for gain, not necessarily associated with wealth. Obsessively erecting boundaries, being overly guarded and extremely withdrawn, Fives position themselves to be protected and preserved beyond what is necessary and even healthy when they're stuck in the grip of greed.

Their detachment from emotions in order to conserve energy can become an excuse to remain disconnected from themselves and others. "I don't need this" and "I can do without that" is a mindset that gives Fives a sense of strength and superiority. Quelling their needs while buffering anything that could possibly put a strain on their stockpile of resources and energy, they feel fortified. When resources such as money, time, and energy are tight, Fives make do instead of reaching out for help. They prefer to live with less than to be dependent on anyone for anything.

They're not stingy just for the sake of it. Fives operate with the mindset that if something has value or they could potentially run out, they may find it useful someday, so they need to hold on to or accumulate it. "I am not a hoarder. I do not enjoy things, but I have five bags of these specific chocolate chips in a drawer at home, and every time I go to the store, I buy another bag so that I won't run out," Elisa, a type Five, told me. Like their fellow head/fear triad type Sixes, the "what if" mindset sets them on a trajectory of fear, as they frantically accumulate both tangible and intangible items "just in case."

While the tangible accumulations, like Elisa's chocolate chips, can certainly be a trap for Fives, oftentimes the *real* snare is the idolatry of the intangible. Minimalist by nature, you won't typically meet a Five who is a hoarder or greedy for material gain. Rather, it's the intangible they accumulate: knowledge, time, and energy. Idolatry makes no distinction over the tangible versus intangible: anything we seek, desire, crave, choose, or pursue over the Creator is idolatrous. The first commandment given in Exodus 20:3 explicitly addresses idolatry: "You shall have no other gods before me." Refining the human heart of idolatry is foundational and fundamental because when sufficiency is found in yourself, the perception is that your need for a Savior is negated.

The core fear behind behaviors associated with avarice is insufficiency, but the root of the sin is pride. The pride of self-sufficiency is the idea that one is capable of creating their own world, where they are not constrained or confined, defenseless to or dependent on anyone.

With any sin, the desire behind the sin isn't always inherently wrong or bad. Often they are normal, human desires and, in fact, sometimes they are *good*. It's what we do with the desires that dictates the destination and where those desires land us.

What we fix our eyes upon is what we focus our hearts on. Eve saw the forbidden fruit, she desired it, and she took it. David saw the beautiful Bathsheba, he desired her and took her. When Fives are fixated on things they lack, needs that may not be met, or threats to their resources, they feed their fear of insufficiency.

In Luke 12:15, Jesus prefaced the parable of the rich fool by warning the people in the crowd: "Take care, and be on your guard against all covetousness, for one's life does not consist in the abundance of his possessions." The Greek word for "abundance" here is *perisseuo*, which contains the idea of exceeding, surpassing, having a surplus or overflow; more than enough.[1]

What a gracious and generous God—our life isn't reduced to what we possess or don't possess. Our life consists of so much more. In a beautiful benediction, Paul wrote at the end of Ephesians 3, proclaiming, "Now to Him who is able to do far more abundantly beyond all that we ask or think, according to the power that works within us" (3:20 NASB). The word used here for "abundantly beyond" is slightly different than the word Jesus used in Luke 12:15. The Greek word is *huperekperissou*, which contains a prefix that intensifies the meaning of *perisseuo*, adding the idea of being far above, exhaustive, beyond what is able to be measured, or superabundantly.[2]

Virtue and Essence: Transparency and Openhandedness

When spiritually aligned, Fives live openhandedly and transparently. Not to be confused with honesty and candidness, transparency isn't simply the lack of pretense—fives can't stand inauthenticity or insincerity. While the virtue of transparency does entail allowing motives, thoughts, or needs to be more easily perceived than what comes naturally, the heart of it speaks to the transparency of a material object—something that allows the light to shine through.

To the extent that we allow ourselves to be seen and our needs known, that is the extent to which we allow the light of Christ to shine in and through us, illuminating his all-sufficiency and provision. When Fives are rooted in the sufficiency of Christ, trusting that he is enough, they are freed from the fear of being left utterly depleted and no longer feel compelled to conceal and control their resources or what they share with others. The Fives' journey of transparency beckons them to be forthcoming, offering their time, intellect, and—most importantly—themselves when they otherwise may not bother. Intimacy in trusted relationships is simply "in-to-me-you-see," as our mentors, Jeff and Lora, taught me and my husband early in our marriage. The trust that transparency necessitates is fundamental to adopting the posture of open hands.

Transparency will require work for the Five in both the physical and mental realms. For those of us with Fives in our lives, we will need to ask them questions directly and they will need to commit to answering and engaging, even when it takes a physical and mental toll. To put it frankly, we have a responsibility to ask, but Fives have a responsibility to answer to cultivate Christian community.

Community is a transparency practice field for Fives. The traditional church small group may feel like a soul-sucking experience even for those Fives who desire to engage and grow spiritually. Finding a few people they can commit to engaging with transparently, with clear spiritual direction, will yield more fruit in the life of a Five than eight weeks in a workbook with a larger group. Like stained glass windows, a Five's beauty is illuminated to its fullness only when the light shines through. However, allowing the light to shine through requires transparency instead of disconnected detachment.

As a type Eight, I go to a Five in times of stress. For instance, the day I went into labor with my son, I found myself detached and disconnected from all emotion. Almost four weeks before my due date, I hadn't *planned* on giving birth that day, and there was quite a bit I had not finished up to prepare for maternity leave—on top of the fact that no one really *plans* to have a pre-term baby. I spent the afternoon and evening with the contraction monitor on my belly, using my makeshift standing desk of the hospital bedside table to make finals edits to the proposal for this book, talking on the phone with Meredith Brock—my incredible literary agent—and texting my mom updates and telling her what I needed from home.

My labor continued, ending in a failed attempt to flip my breech boy, a scary drop in his heart rate, and an emergency C-section I had done everything in my power to avoid. It was not lost on me as I lay there on the operating room table, arms stretched out to either side, palms up, that I was about to receive the greatest gift of my life. But I was only going to receive him by relinquishing my tight grasp of control and surrendering to a C-section.

The posture of openhandedness forces us to relinquish what we hold dearest (time, energy, resources, relationships) in a position of offering, with our palms up. And it's that exact posture that allows us to receive more than we could ask for or imagine. When Fives open their hands and trade their scarcity mindset for surrender, they are able to receive the abundance that awaits.

For the Five, dealing with the core emotion of fear, overcoming the scarcity mindset, and living transparently all boil down to being intentionally generous. Not grabbing and holding on, but offering up to others. There is enough because Christ is enough. Open your hands and receive.

How to Grow as a Type Five

Silence

The spiritual practice of silence brings type Fives to a centered place where they can appropriately detach from what they are holding on to and instead offer generously, with open hands, all they have to God and to others. Silence is the perfect counterbalancing practice for all the ideas circulating in and mental constructs of a Five's mind. As a Five, the idea of silence as a spiritual practice may sound exhilarating—being away from the noise and busyness, alone perhaps. But the space of silence is not for the purpose of filling it with more thought and mental activity. It's for quieting the mind so that the voice of truth can be heard. The voice of truth that says their needs are not a problem or imposition because there is enough—Christ is enough. Silence recenters type Fives to a place of enoughness.

Connect to Your Feelings

Engaging the silence is what helps the Five connect to their feelings and their body. Since Fives often describe needing to think about their feelings, utilizing a feelings chart may help them more readily identify, access, and engage with their emotions. Chip Dodd, a counselor and the author who formulated The Eight Feelings construct in his book *The Voice of the Heart*, created a chart with the eight core emotions.[3] He outlines the impairment of these feelings, which happens when we attempt to avoid vulnerability by blocking them, as well as the gift the eight emotions bring when they are willingly engaged through patience, work, and time.

Impairment	Truth	Gift
Resentment	HURT	Healing and Courage
Apathy	LONELY	Intimacy
Self-pity	SAD	Acceptance
Depression	ANGER	Passion
Anxiety	FEAR	Wisdom and Faith
Toxic shame and Contempt	SHAME	Humility
Toxic shame and Pride	GUILT	Freedom and Forgiveness
Sensuous or sensual pleasure without heart	GLAD	Joy with sadness

This tool can be hugely helpful for those in the head triad, especially the type Five, to connect their head to their heart. Save an image of the feelings chart on your phone, or jot down the eight core emotions in a notes app, and access this information regularly to identify what you're feeling, better engage your emotions, and begin sharing them with others.

Journaling with pen and paper about your emotions will bring them to the surface as you engage in the tactile act of writing, which slows the cadence of the mind and helps you connect with your body. Here are a few journal prompts you may find helpful:

- What are you afraid to open your hands and let go of? How is that fear driving your decisions? What could you receive if your hands were empty and open?
- What feelings do you find most confusing? Are there particular emotions you avoid or resist? What are the benefits and gifts of these emotions?
- Beyond material possessions, how have others been generous to you? What did you feel as the recipient of their generosity? In what ways can you show generosity to someone else?

Connect to Your Body

Staying connected to your body helps with engaging in experiences rather than remaining a spectator. For Fives, this may mean practicing yoga, taking a dance class, or trying your hand at gardening or building something instead of just reading about it or discussing it. When you find yourself withdrawing to observe from the sidelines, use that opportunity to step in and practice engaging your body, your emotions, and other people. Since actively engaging may sound exhausting, schedule time on your calendar for it, whether with another person or doing an activity alone.

Connect with Others

Like the process of procuring the precious oil from olives, when Fives express themselves through journaling or talking with others, everything they have kept pent up is shared, and it's a rich gift to those who receive it. Not every activity must have the prerequisite of increasing your knowledge or competence, or of being productive. Spiritual-growth practices are never a waste of time. They can soften the overly fortified soul of a Five and make them a more connected, compassionate, and engaged human being instead of a spectator. Take it on faith, Fives: it doesn't have to be "educational" to be important. Tell yourself that what you're doing is useful, and in time you will believe it is true.

Training your body and mind will be important in your spiritual-growth journey. Reminding yourself that you can do anything for a little while will give you the perspective and push needed to engage when you'd prefer to opt out. While the thought of all the energy required to engage relationally may cause you to feel physically ill at times, two actions will help: keeping your body well hydrated and rested and keeping your mind clear by minimizing processed sugar and excessive caffeine. If you are going into a social setting or small group, remember that it won't last forever, and participating won't kill you.

Fives, you have enough, even when you don't think you do. You have enough energy, you have enough resources, you have enough knowledge. But that awareness alone isn't enough, because you can't think your way into transformation. Transformation happens through the experience of living. The spiritual journey is filled with people and practices because that is where life is lived, among people and through engagement. That's where change is experienced and transformation happens.

REMEMBER

You will have enough.

READ

"My son, do not forget my teaching,
but let your heart keep my commandments,
for length of days and years of life
and peace they will add to you.
Let not steadfast love and faithfulness forsake you;
bind them around your neck;
write them on the tablet of your heart.
So you will find favor and good success
in the sight of God and man.
Trust in the LORD with all your heart,
and do not lean on your own understanding.
In all your ways acknowledge him,
and he will make straight your paths.
Be not wise in your own eyes;
fear the LORD, and turn away from evil.
It will be healing to your flesh
and refreshment to your bones.
Honor the LORD with your wealth
and with the firstfruits of all your produce;
then your barns will be filled with plenty,
and your vats will be bursting with wine." (Proverbs 3:1–10)

"Such is the confidence that we have through Christ toward God. Not that we are sufficient in ourselves to claim anything as coming from us, but our sufficiency is from God, who has made us sufficient to be ministers of a new covenant, not of the letter but of the Spirit. For the letter kills, but the Spirit gives life." (2 Corinthians 3:4–6)

"My son, if you accept my words
  and store up my commands within you,
  turning your ear to wisdom
  and applying your heart to understanding—
  indeed, if you call out for insight
  and cry aloud for understanding,
  and if you look for it as for silver
  and search for it as for hidden treasure,
  then you will understand the fear of the LORD
  and find the knowledge of God.
  For the LORD gives wisdom;
  from his mouth come knowledge and understanding."
    (Proverbs 2:1–6 NIV)

RESPOND

- Start to see where the scarcity mentality sneaks up, and practice surrendering and resting in the sufficiency of Christ.
- Offer information to others without being asked. The practice of opening your hands will help ingrain this counterintuitive posture into your heart.
- Learning comes through living. Remember this when you feel yourself trying to think your way into transformation.
- Engage and interact with others instead of retreating into the recesses of your mind. Accessing your emotions builds empathy, and conversations can converge in mutual compassion.
- Participate in the everyday wonder and adventure of your own life. Spectating, though safer, will never satisfy.

11

TYPE SIX:

FAITH AND COURAGE

THE TYPE SIX, THE LOYALISTS, CAN BE TRULY altruistic humans whose actions align with what is most advantageous for the greatest number of people. Devoted, dependable, and dutiful, Sixes show up and stick it out even when things get tough. Their commitment in relationships and to institutions remains steadfast through all seasons; once they commit, reneging isn't a consideration. Fiercely protective and loyal to the end, anyone fortunate enough to have a Six in their corner will likely never know a more faithful friend.

The virtue that type Sixes embody is faith. This faith is in no way flippant but rather a hard-won faith that anchors them amid anxiety. When faith is practiced, courage abounds. The courage that emerges isn't mustered up: it's a by-product of belief, a confidence in what is hoped for and assurance in what is unseen (Hebrews 11:1). The spiritual work of the Six is to cast all their cares on the Lord who cares for them (1 Peter 5:7). This practice enables Sixes to silence the worry that seeks to overtake their minds and instead stand on their firmly rooted faith, where they find ultimate safety and security.

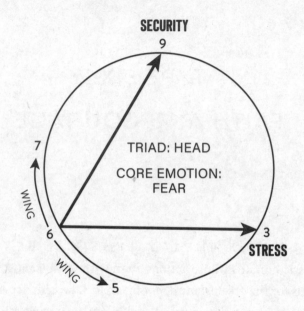

The Fear Triad

Situated squarely in the fear triad and flanked by the type Five and type Seven, Sixes find themselves surrounded with fear as their sin tendency and as their core emotion. Also known as the head-centered or thinking triad, Sixes in this group make certain of their own preservation with contingency plans. Fearing that they may appear—or even worse, actually *be*—incompetent, they experience inner conflict when trying to prove to themselves that they are capable of doing the things they think they cannot.

Sixes do not instinctively trust themselves; doing so is not only counterintuitive, but it also feels *wrong*. They may believe they are inherently bad or evil and therefore incapable of producing anything good, stable, or secure. This can be compounded for the Sixes who grew up in a religious system where fear was misused as a tactic to bring about certain behaviors or rein in unwanted ones. Preying on followers by utilizing the powerful emotion of fear, these types of organizations and churches attempt to ensure their ideas and standards are abided by.

Understandably, Sixes sometimes have issues with authority. Early on, they picked up on the message that authority figures— maybe a parent, teacher, or pastor—couldn't be trusted, which propelled them into a deep dependency on authority figures as they searched for one who could and would protect them because they see themselves as weak and afraid. Conversely, this mistrust may have served to push them against authority figures, rebelling against anyone who sought to exploit their weakness and fear and use it against them.

"Sometimes [fear] looks like being suspicious of others' motives and refusing to trust the people close to me because I'm scared of being vulnerable and getting hurt," Brigitta, a type Six, shared. This is a common experience for many Sixes, resulting in anxiety over things they cannot control—which is everyone and everything but themselves and their response/actions. This presents a predicament for Sixes. They are suspicious of others' motives and don't feel as though it's safe to trust those in authority. But they are equally self-doubting, which activates their anxiety and can keep them stuck, unable to make a decision and move forward.

Decision paralysis is a common experience for the fear triad but especially plagues Sixes because they always want to ensure they are choosing the right, best, or safest option and thus they stall out. The time that elapses while Sixes are stuck in decision paralysis conjures up self-doubt. When they get stuck in an unhealthy place of fear and indecision, it becomes a vicious cycle, where they seek more guidance and ask more questions, stockpiling information that they never apply to the decision. They don't make a decision, which ironically compounds their fear and inability to decide.

Sam, a type Six, knew it was time to look for a new job. She loved the organization she worked for, their mission and the work they were doing within the city, but it had taken its toll on her in every way. Being responsible and reliable, she was the person things fell to when a crisis erupted. Continually being understaffed contributed to her burnout; she was depleted and done. It created tremendous turmoil within her for months as her loyalty prevented her from leaving the organization. She was stuck in decision paralysis. The mountain seemed insurmountable; everything felt impossible. But then one day, she decided. After months of deliberation, she told me that she was leaving and taking a new job. She spoke with such assurance and clarity, it was almost as if I were talking to a totally different person from the girl who had been stuck in a frenzy of fear for so many months. No longer spinning out in "what ifs" or stuck in decision paralysis, she was steady instead of self-doubting.

This is a strange crossroads, where self-doubt and self-sufficiency intersect for the type Six. In the fear triad, self-sufficiency manifests in their pursuits of acquiring information (Fives), creating experiences (Sevens), and seeking safety (Sixes). If Fives can acquire enough information, if Sevens can have enough thrilling experiences, if Sixes can create safety and security, then they will be okay. "It feels like I'm looking for security but at the same time doubting that God is the one who can provide that in my life. So, I look to other things/people for support or guidance," Brigitta went on to share about the struggles of self-doubt as a Six.

Their self-sufficiency in creating safe and secure circumstances (which is merely an illusion) combines with the self-doubt that they do not have the resources, knowledge, skill set, or strength to survive whatever comes. This is where the virtue of faith and essence of courage for the type Six arises. Self-sufficiency is replaced with the sufficiency of Christ by the work of redemption that was finished on the cross. Self-doubt is swallowed up by faith because his promises are true, and nothing rests on us or hinges on our ability or strength.

Sin Proclivity: Fear

Sixes have a complicated relationship with fear. For people in recovery or who are part of a twelve-step program, sobriety is a key component of their journey, which requires abstinence from the substance that led to addiction or abuse. But there are other patterns of addiction, known as process addictions or behavioral addictions, where the compulsion is to engage consistently in an activity or behavior rather than a substance.[1] Process addictions can include food, sex, shopping, and relationships, to name a few. The kicker with process addictions, unlike substance addiction, is that total abstinence from the process isn't always possible.

For those who have struggled with an eating disorder, like

me, you can't go the rest of your life without eating food. For many who find themselves perpetually in codependent relationships, they cannot cut themselves off from human connection altogether, since relationships are our lifeblood. For those in recovery from a sex addiction, the solution is not a life of celibacy, because we were created for intimacy, including physical and sexual intimacy. The process or behavior that has led down a path of destruction isn't inherently bad or sinful, but it's a stumbling block. This is the predicament of fear for the Six: it's a lifesaving emotion yet it also entraps and entangles them.

For Sixes, fear can be the life preserver that saves them or the millstone that drowns them. Fear isn't sin, and being fearful isn't sinful. Fear is an emotion and emotions are a human experience; they are amoral. But when fear gets distorted, it becomes an obsession. Fear turns to obsessive worry over what cannot be controlled. Sixes find a false sense of security in the cycle of obsession, believing that planning can modify and mitigate. When fear becomes an obsession, it can result in a lack of trust, where compulsion is stronger than courage and fear outpaces faith. This is where anxiety enters the equation, warping the primal emotion that was given to us as a guide.

Before diving too much deeper here, I want to be clear that being anxious, having an anxiety disorder, and/or taking medication for anxiety are *not* sins. As I'm writing this book, I am five months postpartum and working with my midwife, a counselor, and a naturopathic doctor to address depression and anxiety unlike any I have ever experienced. Anxiety can have organic causes. An organic disease is defined as "a disease in which anatomic or pathophysiology changes occur in some body tissue or organ," including our brains and bodies when they're hijacked by anxiety.[2] Anxiety is not a result of some unconfessed sin in your life. However, anxiety can lead us to live a life where we engage in behaviors and coping mechanisms that are not in alignment with what God has for us. Can anxiety manifest because of our sinful choices or lifestyle? Yes. But it cannot be distilled down to a simple cause-and-effect relationship.

"When it comes to my relationship with fear and anxiety, it's as if my mind wants to extrapolate all of the negative possibility of any given situation so that I'm not caught off guard or unprepared. I often feel that if I can brace myself for tragedy, it won't hurt as much," Cam, a type Six, remarked. While being prepared is wise, Cam articulated where Sixes slip into unhelpful catastrophic thinking that propels them toward worry. Even while knowing on a cognitive level that bracing for tragedy by forecasting for catastrophe will not, in fact, lessen the pain, Sixes still try to prepare by employing this kind of thinking.

My high school counselor who introduced me to the Enneagram, Sissy Goff, would regularly talk about anxiety in our Thursday night girls' group. Anxiety, as she explained, is an overestimation of the threat and an underestimation of our ability to cope. In overestimating the threats facing us, whether real or perceived, we learned that we were allowing our anxiety to steer us by self-sabotaging and forecasting for catastrophe. In an attempt to control our circumstances or not be caught off guard when the unexpected happens, these tactics, which seem like they may be of service, are actually snares to living in freedom and trust.

Anxiety predominantly arises in type Sixes when they try to *ensure* safety and security. While there are plenty of things that one can try to guarantee, the biggest, most anxiety-producing elements in life can never be ensured. The motivation for safety isn't bad—it's good and pure, and healthy fear is often what protects us from catastrophic harm. But forecasting for catastrophic outcomes can give Sixes a false sense of security, and in an attempt to fortify themselves, they inadvertently confine themselves to fear. Ruminating on the worst-case scenario instead of courageously taking action is what stalls out Sixes in sinful patterns.

Forecasting for catastrophic outcomes, as if you have complete control as long as you have enough resources and time to plan and prepare, only leads to worsening anxiety (sideways fear) and crippling busyness, which expends all of your physical and mental energy. The mere suggestion of something potentially threatening that is not according to the plan can cause Sixes to jump to distrust and then down the rabbit hole. The sad result of this downward spiral of never-ending, nondirectional busyness is a lonely, dark jail cell of fear. When this happens, Sixes fail to flex their muscles of faith to build and strengthen them.

Virtue and Essence: Faith and Courage

On the type Sixes' journey of spiritual transformation, the virtue of faith and the essence of courage go hand in hand. The essence of courage *is* faith—the assurance of things hoped for and conviction of things unseen (Hebrews 11:1). Instead of frantically seeking proof, embracing the mystery of faith is the journey. Courage cannot be mustered or bootstrapped. It's the by-product of consistently placing your confidence in Christ alone.

We love an empowering and energizing "faith over fear" or "be strong and have courage" tagline. But faith isn't simply about facing fear. Fear isn't something to be conquered. No amount of faith will extinguish the fiery fear common to the human experience. Fear is one of the most primal protective instincts. It's a life-preserving emotion that shields you from harm and is a safeguard against pain. If pain didn't exist, you wouldn't stop touching the hot stove. Fear of the hot stove is the safeguard against being burned.

Like all emotions, fear is real and valid, but one's life cannot be built on emotions. Feelings will shift and change as circumstances influence them. The stove in and of itself isn't something to be feared. Sure, when it's hot it would be wise to approach it with caution, but when it's off, there is no reason to fear it.

Faith can and will triumph over fear, but for Sixes, this requires them to trade in their wavering faith for a sure and secure anchor for their soul. A foundation of faith is unmoving amid the fluctuating circumstances. Sixes can be comforted by the truth found in 2 Timothy 2:13, that even "if [or *when*] we are faithless, he remains faithful—for he cannot deny himself."

All the Sixes are probably asking, "Yeah, okay, but how do I do this?" There's good news and bad news. I'll start with the bad news: you don't have the ability on your own. And that's also the good news, the best news we could have hoped for. Nothing about the gospel has to do with what we can do, what we bring to the table, what we're able to muster up or bootstrap. We can do nothing on our own strength.

It's not in our ability: it's in our choice to place our faith in Christ alone. That's really at the heart of what courage is—it's a choice we make repeatedly. It's not a one-and-done but rather a daily decision to trust and to take the scary next step. That's courage: waking up another day and saying, "Yes, Lord." Faith begins with fragile and faltering first steps, and courage comes from consistent choices. Faith is the first step in the journey of transformation, and true spiritual transformation is the Six's only hope to show up in the world courageously.

In 2 Timothy 1:7 we read these encouraging words: "for God gave us a spirit not of fear but of power and love and self-control." Most days it won't *feel* that way, as fear creeps in and the "what ifs" start to fly. But what hope and peace this verse brings. Our right standing with God doesn't mean that we won't stumble and sin. It does mean that we don't have to perpetually strive to earn our seat at the table. It's been given to us already—our seat is saved, reserved with a place card bearing our name.

In the same way, we don't have to strive for the courage to overcome fear or for power over timidity—they have already been *given* to us. Power, love, and self-discipline were granted to us, bestowed upon us. That is a tremendous source of comfort and hope because when you've come to the end of yourself and realize you can do nothing to earn, attain, or acquire, you humbly open your hands to receive what has already been given to you. God put a spirit of *power* within the hearts of his people. He has given us a spirit of love, *his love*, which is perfect and casts out fear (1 John 4:18).

Self-discipline for Sixes requires them to confront fears that turn into timidity: acknowledge the fear and the way it's trying to save, help, or protect them, and then appropriately arrange it in its place in the back seat of the car, not the driver's seat. Fear can guide and serve you if you don't allow it to control your conscious mind and drive your decisions, which is possible through self-discipline. Self-discipline, though simple, cannot be equated with easy. For Sixes, the practices of silence, meditation, and grounding keep them out of the frenzied franticness of fear. However, choosing to engage in these practices instead of allowing the mind to run untamed requires tremendous self-discipline.

How to Grow as a Type Six

Silence

The spiritual practice of silence is the hallmark practice for the fear triad (types Five, Six, and Seven). Silence for Sixes is both internal and external. Limiting their environmental and external stimuli—especially their intake of news and current events, podcasts, shows, music, and chatter—helps them begin to silence their hearts and minds. Turning down the physical noise is part of the equation, but silencing their minds is the real work for Sixes. Most people wouldn't guess at their inner turmoil or the prison the competent, capable Sixes' minds can become when fixated on fears and anxiously assessing all that is around them.

Sixes' brains are like a web browser with tabs open to infinity and beyond. Living with their screen split, one half tries to work and function, while the other half constantly flashes with potential hazards and problematic situations: the smoke detector batteries that need to be changed, the weather radar that needs to be checked to see if the severity of the storm predicted has increased, the black mold that could be lurking in the home, the stock market that is becoming increasing volatile, and the list goes on. This is part of how they're wired, and over the years I've come to see that a lot of our wiring, instead of being "good" or "bad," simply *is*. And rather than white-knuckling it and fighting it, learning to utilize and harness it is the work at hand.

"I have found that utilizing my very visual brain helps me

to process those things. By visualizing my thoughts, I'm able to see myself interact with them, organize them, and even overcome them," said Cam about his experience as a type Six. Instead of trying to force his mind, he uses the visual and imaginative components to organize and interact with his thoughts and ideas rather than being controlled by and confined to them. Sixes are verbal processors, and while this can require their partners, friends, and colleagues to be patient, it is a practice that can help them appropriately acknowledge their fears in a way that leads them to *action.*

The wild imagination of a Six is both a powerful asset and their weak point. "I've realized that my own mind is both a terrifying place and a sanctuary. It's full of things I fear and don't trust. Many times, it's easy to shut off my mind so I don't have to deal with things like anxiety and trauma," Cam added.

Harness the power of your imagination. Think through what all could go wrong, while carefully and mindfully looking at the worst-case scenario. Then imagine the best possible outcome, the ten out of ten, better than you could have ever hoped. Realize that reality will fall somewhere in the middle. Don't give too much power to the worst while failing to consider the best.

Meditation

Meditation is a powerful practice for all types but especially the head-centered types. Meditation arrests the frantic frenzy of the mind by forcing an external stimulus on it to slow it down and silence the noise. There are myriad apps out there (Headspace, Abide, and Insight Timer, to name a few), but it can also be as simple as turning on some instrumental music and reading line by line, word by word, a certain passage of Scripture (see the end of this chapter for some passages for your Six soul). This practice stills the mind in the moment but also equips you with tools for the fight, an arsenal of Scripture committed to memory, to recall when the battle in your mind begins to wage.

Self-doubt will tag along, but ignoring it will not silence it. Keep an index card or a small notebook at hand and when you feel the self-doubt start to shout in your mind, stop and write it down. Write down what doubt is speaking to you and then counter it with an affirmation or truth. "When self-doubt says, 'You're not good enough' or 'You'll fail,' I remind myself that God's love for me is not based on my performance and that I'm really good at my job," said Sammie, a type Six. She went on to say that after having lived abroad and moving many times for her work, that "every time I move I self-doubt that I'll be able to make friends or that anyone will like me . . . I remind myself of all the moves before and all the people and close friends God has blessed me with." When self-doubt springs up, it's a great time to employ the Scripture you have committed to memory through meditation. Isaiah 41:10 is densely packed with truth to quell self-doubt: "Fear not, for I am with you; be not dismayed, for I am your God; I will strengthen you, I will help you, I will uphold you with my righteous right hand."

Journaling

Forcing the frenzy of fear in your mind to a halt, the natural cadence of writing down one thought, one idea, one word at a time helps Sixes. When Sixes slow down their thoughts, they can get out of their heads and into their hearts and bodies, to feel and sense what is going on inside them. Here are some journal prompts that may be helpful as a jumping-off place:

- What situation in your life is currently causing you stress and anxiety? Instead of focusing on the worst-case scenario, what is the best possible outcome?
- Where is self-doubt keeping you confined from living as you were created to, in freedom? Is self-doubt stopping you from being obedient, even in small ways, today?
- Think about a time when you acted boldly or courageously. What did you do or say? What obstacles did you have to overcome? How did you feel? What did it take to get there? You are a master at planning—now make a plan to re-create that behavior the next time courage is required.

Stay in the Present

Grounding yourself in the present helps you not jump headlong down the rabbit hole. Instead of looking down the road, anticipating all the possible problems that could arise, look back on all the ways God has remained faithful, every time he has met you perfectly in your time of need. Lamentations 3:21–23 is a powerful passage to memorize: "But this I call to mind, and therefore I have hope: The steadfast love of the LORD never ceases; his mercies never come to an end; they are new every morning; great is your faithfulness."

I would be remiss to conclude this chapter without acknowledging the "what ifs" that may be spinning up and contingencies and caveats that may be forming in your mind, even after exploring faith, courage, and how to grow as a type Six. I know this truth will feel terrifying, but you are strong enough to handle and hear this: Jesus is the only one you can count on. People will betray you. They will take advantage of you, they will mislead you (sometimes intentionally but other times unintentionally), they can't always be trusted, they will fail you, and they will leave you. But *he* will never leave or forsake you (Joshua 1:9).

For Sixes who have committed Joshua 1:9 to memory as a weapon for war when the fear closes in—by focusing on the "be strong and courageous" part—also focus and meditate on the second half: "the LORD your God is with you wherever you go." That is where your strength and hope lie. Not in your own courage and strength but in the truth that surely he is with you always, to the very end of the age (Matthew 28:20).

REMEMBER

You are safe and held.

READ

"I sought the Lord, and he answered me
and delivered me from all my fears." (Psalm 34:4)

"If any of you lacks wisdom, let him ask God, who gives generously to all without reproach, and it will be given him. But let him ask in faith, with no doubting, for the one who doubts is like a wave of the sea that is driven and tossed by the wind." (James 1:5–6)

"Therefore do not be anxious, saying, 'What shall we eat?' or 'What shall we drink?' or 'What shall we wear?' For the Gentiles seek after all these things, and your heavenly Father knows that you need them all. But seek first the kingdom of God and his righteousness, and all these things will be added to you. Therefore do not be anxious about tomorrow, for tomorrow will be anxious for itself. Sufficient for the day is its own trouble." (Matthew 6:31–34)

RESPOND

- Learn to distinguish between legitimate fear and the hamster wheel of worry. If it's worry, arrest it. If it's fear, does it require an action or response?
- Notice where self-doubt is disabling you. Take a step into confidence—your competence and capability will have your back.
- Remember that the ultimate work is not to establish safety and security at every point but rather to embrace the wild adventure of a life of faith.
- Vulnerability is a practice you will need to engage in regularly with select people. While few individuals are as loyal and dependable as you, that doesn't mean there aren't trustworthy people who want to love you.
- When you find yourself making a contingency plan or asking, "Yeah, but what if . . . ?" notice where fear is doing its job of keeping you safe and thank it, but move forward without being constrained by it or confined to it.

12

TYPE SEVEN: WISDOM AND SOBRIETY

TYPE SEVENS, THE ADVENTURERS, HAVE A PLAYFUL presence and optimistic outlook on life. Their spontaneous and whimsical way of engaging every day brings dazzling delight to anyone fortunate enough to know them. Looking at the world with wide-eyed enthusiasm and having seemingly endless energy, Sevens are explorers and experience seekers. Versatile and flexible, Sevens keep their options open and their opportunities flowing.

Spiritually aligned Sevens exude joy, but unlike their happy-go-lucky cadence, this joy is deeply anchored and is developed when they have confronted the painful parts of life. When spiritually grounded and engaged, Sevens are thoughtful and intentional with wisdom, which is their virtue, as their guide into a more metered way of living.

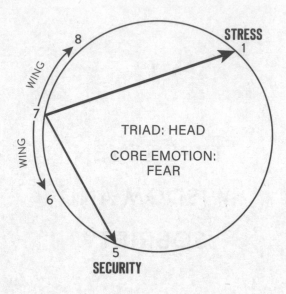

The Fear Triad

Rounding out the head-centered or thinking triad, along with types Five and Six, the core emotion of the Seven is fear. In the same way Nines are somewhat oblivious to their anger, when I asked a type Seven about her experience with fear, she said, "Hmm, let me think about that and get back to you." Though fear feels like a foreigner to Sevens, it is closer than they may know.

What Sevens fear on a visceral level is being trapped. They can expend enormous amounts of time and energy avoiding painful experiences, relationships, and circumstances. They fear boredom, being lonely, not being taken care of, or being left destitute. Their fear of being trapped or bored can lead to them perpetually seeking mountaintop experiences to avoid pain, often resulting in the sin of gluttony, where enough is never enough.

Scarcity mindset can be a major struggle for the type Seven, as it flows from their fear of being deprived. This fear of deprivation can compound their bent toward gluttony. When they fall into a scarcity mindset, they become almost manic consumers, gathering, gleaning, accumulating, hoarding, and fiercely holding on to what they can grasp. This can often be in the form of relationships, information, and experiences.

Coupled with a scarcity mindset and fear of being trapped, the mere thought of living an ordinary life is enough to cause a Seven to have a mental breakdown. "I'm afraid of being trapped inside a completely ordinary life, where nothing is really bad but also nothing is really good or exciting. It's just ordinary," explained Faulkner, a type Seven. Sevens live with perpetual FOMO (fear of missing out)—not so much the fear of missing out on the weekend party or upcoming event but the fear of missing out on life itself. This can affect their decisions on both a daily and long-term basis. They are seekers of the extraordinary in order to avoid the painful boredom and humdrum of the ordinary.

In the play *Our Town* by Thornton Wilder, the first act, titled "Daily Life," chronicles a normal happening in the fictional small town of Grover's Corners in the early 1900s. With the milkman making deliveries and the paperboy on his morning route, families are awakening to the day, eating breakfast, and shuffling children off to school. Emily Webb, one of the main characters, is a girl when the play begins. The scenes follow her through her school years; falling in love with her childhood friend and high school sweetheart, George Gibbs; marrying him; and then tragically dying during childbirth.

The final scene takes place in the graveyard where Emily has just been buried, accompanied by the spirits of other deceased

Grover's Corners citizens. The Stage Manager, who serves as the play's narrator, tells Emily that though she can return to the past and relive one of her days, he advises against it because she will surely be disappointed. Even so, he urges her to choose an unimportant day, lest it be too painful for her to revisit the past. She settles on her twelfth birthday.

Returning to that day, she comes downstairs to the breakfast table, where she joins her father, mother, and younger brother. An ordinary morning on another ordinary day, but from her perspective now, nothing is ordinary. It's as if, for the first time, she realizes how beautiful and meaningful her life was. It's colored with the brilliance of everyday moments she never stopped to notice while they were happening.

"Oh, Mama, just look at me one minute as though you really saw me . . . Mama, just for a moment we're happy. Let's really look at one another!" she cries out.

Turning back to the Stage Manager, she asks to be taken back up the hill to the graveyard. "I can't go on. It goes so fast. We don't have time to look at one another. I didn't realize. So all that was going on and we never noticed."

Afterward, when she returns to her grave, she exclaims,

Wait! One more look. Good-bye, Good-bye world. Good-bye, Grover's Corners . . . Mama and Papa. Good-bye to clocks ticking . . . and Mama's sunflowers. And food and coffee. And new ironed dresses and hot baths . . . and sleeping and waking up.

Upon her return to the graveyard she laments, "Oh, earth, you're too wonderful for anybody to realize you." Then she asks the

Stage Manager, "Do any human beings ever realize life while they live it?—every, every minute?"[1]

For the type Seven, the most perilous trap they can fall into is not savoring life while they live it. With their natural tendency toward future thinking and their quest for adventure paired with their fear of being trapped in a place of painful meaninglessness, they rarely embrace what is ordinary, never realizing the gift of the present. "The grass always seems greener because I haven't put a blanket down in the grass where I'm standing," Jeana explained of her experience as a Seven.

Sevens, in your fear of the ordinary, your fear of missing out, your fear of being trapped, you miss out on the beautiful moments life presents you each day. When looking at the greener grass, you fail to see the vibrant, lush green grass you're already standing on, where you could sit down and enjoy a picnic. Your life is a quest for the extraordinary, but the irony is that you, your life and all that it contains, *is* extraordinary because of the joy within you that enables the rest of us to see the world in technicolor.

Sin Proclivity: Gluttony

The mindset of "more of a good thing is a good thing!" is how most Sevens operate, explained Kelsey, a dear friend and type Seven. "But it can actually be a bad thing," she added. "More is better" is the motto for the Seven who is spiritually tuned out. This arises from their intense need to avoid pain and discomfort. Keeping themselves busy and distracted, Sevens fall prey to overindulging and overdoing, the constant pursuit of more.

It's important to bear in mind what motivates each type to

sin—both their sin proclivity and myriad other sins that entangle and entrap them. Sometimes it's not the desires themselves that are sinful; it's the choice made to fulfill their desires that is sinful. In the garden of Eden, Eve didn't set out to sin. She *desired* something and what she desired wasn't inherently bad. She desired the delight, the food, and the wisdom and knowledge the tree offered: "When the woman saw that the tree was good for food, and that it was a delight to the eyes, and that the tree was desirable to make one wise, she took some of its fruit and ate" (Genesis 3:6 NASB).

Eve's desire for food and wisdom wasn't sinful—the means by which she fulfilled that desire was sinful. She lived in the garden of Eden, in perfect communion with God, who is the source of all wisdom. Yet the serpent promised that she could find wisdom another way. Satan tempted her with the forbidden fruit of the tree as a way to gratify her desire. She had everything she needed, but she still wanted more.

For Sevens, gluttony is rooted in their desire to have enough, to be taken care of, to experience freedom instead of entrapment. Those desires aren't bad; they are a normal part of the human experience. But sin can arise in the way those needs are met, and gluttony enters the equation. Enough is never enough for the Seven, and that's when overindulgence occurs.

For the seven, gluttony can be the typical vices we link to that term: food, sex, drinking. One Seven included scouring houses on Zillow and perpetual job hunting on LinkedIn on her list of vices. Often, though, Sevens can overindulge in more sophisticated and seemingly less harmful things. Work, particularly when born out of their life's calling, or in the ministry or nonprofit space, can complicate this. Being a workaholic, especially in the name of

Jesus or social justice, is often rewarded and esteemed but can negatively impact Sevens' mental health and spiritual growth.

"Bigger, better, more!" is the mantra of the spiritually asleep Seven. Rather than engaging life with a sobriety of mind, they indulge in pleasure so that when an unpleasant moment occurs, the discomfort is muted and they can keep skipping along at their usual carefree pace. Rather than facing the inevitable disappointments and downfalls of life, Sevens are skilled at reframing even the most catastrophic situations. "I try to make even the most mundane thing fun or at least attach something fun to it so I can reframe it," explained Meredyth, a type Seven. "I don't always remember things in the past correctly. I always forget the bad things, and people have to remind me that things didn't quite go like that."

Being future oriented, Sevens often fail to do the things today that will equip them to accomplish their dreams for tomorrow. Though they aren't lazy, they lack the work ethic in the moment needed to match the goal they're chasing. Planning for what's next robs them of the present. Sevens would do well to remember what they have, here and now, was once something they had dreamed about. When you've been given what you once longed for, gratitude is the appropriate response. Practice being in a place of contentment for your present reality.

The quest for freedom for the type Seven catapults them into a lifestyle of continuous consumption. The tragic irony is that the quest actually becomes the prison. They get stuck in the rat race of life, always seeking the next thing—the next accomplishment, the next experience, the next career step, the next vacation. They believe that the next thing will quell their fear of being trapped or stuck, will bring them bliss-filled days and provide the freedom they've longed for. They buy into the lie that infinite freedom, boundless bliss, and eternal ecstasy await, but what they're missing is the gift of the present, the joy that is already theirs, the life happening right in front of them.

Virtue and Essence: Wisdom and Sobriety

The virtue of wisdom blossoms in the Seven who has learned to engage in life with a temperedness. The aim for sobriety as a Seven isn't necessarily in the traditional sense (from alcohol or other substances) but rather a soberness of mind and spirit. Rather than reframing the disappointments, augmenting the ordinary, or amplifying the fun, living soberly requires an acceptance of reality without attempting to alter it.

In stark contrast to the scattered, hyperactive, addictive, and sometimes superficial behaviors that can characterize their lives, the wisdom of a Seven can be seen in a metered way of moving about their life, enjoying without overindulging, where more isn't better and moderation is the main objective. This can emerge only from the Seven who has found comfort and contentment in Christ, who is the eternal and abundant source of everything they will ever need. The wisdom that surfaces from sobriety becomes the timeless gift they offer the world.

Fully attached to God, the true source of wisdom and abundance, Sevens in turn become wise. No longer fragmented, frayed, and fearful, living in a state of perpetual seeking, Sevens affixed to Christ remain constant and steadfast amid any circumstances. When continually supplied by their source of wisdom, discernment develops, which counterbalances their ravenous appetite for the pleasures of life. Actions become wise instead of wild, and intentional instead of impulsive. On their quest to grow spiritually, Proverbs 4:6–7 reassures Sevens that wisdom belongs to them: "Do not forsake her, and she will keep you; love her, and she will guard you. The beginning of wisdom is this: Get wisdom, and whatever you get, get insight."

When they are grounded in the present and spiritually aligned, joy shines forth from the Seven. While joy seems perfectly fitting with their buoyant personalities, this joy is actually a by-product of being present to painful moments. "Long-suffering can tell the world the story of the source of hope," Molly Wilcox wrote.[2] And I would add that joy can do the same.

Being present to pain is what opens us to the presence of joy, the deep and abiding joy that anchors us in all seasons, that in any circumstances allows us to say, "It is well." It's not either-or when it comes to joy and pain—it's both-and. They are not mutually exclusive or inversely related. They directly correlate: the deeper the pain, the more abundant the joy. This doesn't mean that you have to experience some tragic loss or live in a perpetual state of horrific circumstances. It means that you are willing to show up and be present when the discomforts of life descend. It means that you sit still and silent long enough to learn something rather than chasing down the next high or planning the next adventure to help you escape the present pain. That is the work set before you on your spiritual journey: being present to the pain so that you can live fully and abundantly in the joy, which you will radiate to the darkest places of the earth.

Two neighboring Old Testament books, Ezra and Nehemiah, chronicle the return of the Israelites from a seventy-year exile in Babylon, where they had strayed spiritually, to put it mildly. Amid their return to their homeland and the rebuilding of the temple and the walls of Jerusalem, a spiritual rebuilding was simultaneously happening. Though the Israelites faced tremendous political and spiritual opposition during this time of physical rebuilding and spiritual reformation, the temple was completed, the city wall was rebuilt, and the time for celebration was at hand.

On the holy day of celebration, while Ezra read the word of God to the people, they were so deeply moved by their sin, so sincerely repentant that they wept. But Ezra told them, "Go your way. Eat the fat and drink sweet wine and send portions to anyone who has nothing ready, for this day is holy to our Lord. And do not be grieved, for the joy of the LORD is your strength" (Nehemiah 8:10).

What a celebration it must have been for a people who had been exiled but now were home, who had strayed spiritually but were welcomed back. Their joy was made full from the suffering they had experienced, both from their circumstances and their own actions. Joy was abundant amid their pain. Again, as Nehemiah 8:10 says, "The joy of the LORD is your strength." And that source of joy—that strength—is endless. As Psalm 30:5 reminds us, "For his anger is but for a moment, and his favor is for a lifetime. Weeping may tarry for the night, but joy comes with the morning." Joy that emerges from tears is everlasting.

Everlasting joy is at the core of the Seven. On this side of heaven, pain is inescapable, as John 16:22 makes clear: "Therefore you too have grief now; but . . . your heart will rejoice, and no one is going to take your joy away from you" (NASB). Joy belongs to you, Sevens. Disappointment can't dampen it, suffering can't squelch it, boredom won't belittle it. When you have affixed your eyes on Jesus and attached yourself securely to the source of abundance and wisdom, your joy will never be taken away from you.

How to Grow as a Type Seven

Silence

With their affinity for adventure and pursuit of what's next, Sevens can unintentionally engage half-heartedly spiritually. "There is a difference between being interested in multiple things and being too distracted to focus on any one thing," wrote Molly Wilcox.[3] As the hallmark spiritual practice for the Seven, silence gives way to focused attention. "Even if I am not doing anything, I am thinking about everything," Jeana, a type Seven, said. Silencing their mind from the perpetual planning and adventure addiction is the work. While the spiritual practice of silence may allow painful feelings to emerge for type Sevens, it is what brings sobriety and wisdom to their actions, which is evidence of growth.

Being grounded in the present moment, with their attention fixed on the provision that is in front of them, is paramount for the type Seven. Turn the podcast, show, or music off. Get still and read small segments of Scripture, meditating on one verse or word. Meditation on Scripture that speaks to the sufficiency and enoughness of Christ—such as Philippians 4, Ephesians 3:20, and Matthew 6:25–43—can serve to quiet Sevens' anxious minds and still their souls. Prayer can be acutely powerful for them in moments when their minds start to wander. "I turn my mind to prayer when it wants to start thinking about that new idea I had or fantasizing about how I want my life to look in five years, or if I should plan another trip or margarita day soon," Jeana explained.

Meditation and prayer provide a guided, focused effort to not think about anything, so the mind can be silenced and appropriately affixed on Jesus.

Journaling

Journaling is another practice that helps Sevens arrest their fast-paced, future-focused way of moving about life and align themselves in the present. The practice of writing is particularly helpful for types that move fast mentally and physically, because the act of writing words on a page forces the mind and body to slow down and process as they pen each word.

You can use the following prompts to get started:

- What is one thing you are grateful for in this present moment?
- What are you trying to avoid or escape? Is there a situation you are reframing to avoid boredom or pain?
- Are there particular things you are currently overindulging in (work, food, social media, extracurricular activities, alcohol)? Are you trying to medicate something?

These questions may bring a needed silence to your heart, allowing you to reflect on the past and appropriately engage the present. Dwelling on the small, normal, and even mundane things in life can help Sevens downshift from their frenzied, futuristic pace and be present.

Getting still and quiet, being all alone, or pulling out a journal may feel terrifying. Unpleasant moments and memories will arise. But don't be quick to delete the negatives from your memory. You'll delete both good and bad; you can't exclude one from the other. Spend time processing your pain and reach out to invite others into it. Sevens want to be with people, but they don't often let people *be* with them. People don't need the Seven to be "on" all the time and, in fact, like and appreciate the more toned-down version of the type who often defaults to parlor tricks to maintain their "life of the party" persona. And it's imperative for Sevens to have someone to process pain with and to confront difficult emotions and grief. If that's too radical of an idea for you, consider processing your sadness and pain with a professional counselor.

Fasting

As a countering force to gluttony, fasting can be a helpful spiritual practice for the Seven, though not for the purpose of deprivation or as a punishment for gluttony. Fasting awakens your soul to the sufficiency of Christ through the longing it ignites. It's easy to pack our days full of all the comforts life offers, to the point that we've fed, soothed, and coddled every need and utterly squelched our desire for and dependence on God. While fasting doesn't have to be constrained to food, that can be a very physical way to experience the need it creates. Fasting from things we fill our lives with (social media, Netflix, alcohol, sugar, caffeine, weekend activities) frees up our mental margin so we can focus our attention on and turn to God in prayer.

It may be helpful to set boundaries with yourself, bringing in a trusted friend or counselor, to keep you accountable for things you will not do or engage in—not as a means of legalism but rather as safeguards. Sevens have an addictive type of personality and an affinity for more, more, *more*! As you think about the parameters you will set in your life to stay healthy, get specific about how you overindulge in both big and small ways: overconsuming alcohol or drugs; making continuous high risk, high-reward decisions that might border on gambling; or leaving so little margin in your life that you have no room for silence or self-care.

The spiritual disciplines that are the growth catalyst for the type Seven feel just like that: *discipline*. But practicing them consistently will make the experience less painful, and it will get easier in time. The reward is rich for those willing to walk the road of faith. Believing and trusting in the sufficiency and abundance of Christ is the journey for the Seven. "God will supply every need of yours according to his riches in glory in Christ Jesus," Philippians 4:19 reminds us. In Christ, there is no need, no lacking, no insufficiency—only enough, only abundance, only sufficiency. Scarcity is not your story; abundance is yours in Christ.

REMEMBER

Your needs will be taken care of.

READ

"Not that I am speaking of being in need, for I have learned in whatever situation I am to be content. I know how to be brought low, and I know how to abound. In any and every circumstance, I have learned the secret of facing plenty and hunger, abundance and need. I can do all things through him who strengthens me." (Philippians 4:11–13)

"Dear friends, do not be surprised at the fiery ordeal that has come on you to test you, as though something strange were happening to you. But rejoice inasmuch as you participate in the sufferings of Christ, so that you may be overjoyed when his glory is revealed." (1 Peter 4:12–13 NIV)

"Consider it pure joy, my brothers and sisters, whenever you face trials of many kinds, because you know that the testing of your faith produces perseverance. Let perseverance finish its work so that you may be mature and complete, not lacking anything." (James 1:2–4 NIV)

RESPOND

- When an opportunity or invitation presents itself, take a breath before you agree, set your phone down before you respond, and practice restraint so that you can mindfully say no if needed or wholeheartedly say yes.
- It's okay to dream about the future and fantasize about all the possibilities, but put your feet on the ground, take a deep breath, and bring yourself back into the present moment. It's a gift you don't want to miss out on.
- If you've never met with a counselor or been in therapy, schedule an appointment and don't cancel it. Everyone has unprocessed pain, and you can't run from yours forever. There are skilled professionals who can guide you. You won't drown in the pain, I promise.
- The next time you feel pain or experience discomfort, even if it's by proxy from someone else sharing theirs, practice just being present to it, not reframing it to create a cheap silver lining.
- When you commit, specify a length of time and hold yourself accountable to it. Show up to your small group each week for the next six months. Stick with your job for at least two years. There is great reward in playing the long game and richness found in commitment.

PART THREE

Coming Home

13

THE PATHWAY
TO SPIRITUAL
TRANSFORMATION

DURING MY TIME AT ONSITE, THE PROGRAM
I spoke about earlier in the book, there were many transformative moments, but one remains clear in my mind. The proprietor
and chairman, Miles Adcox, spoke on the opening night to the
group of forty participants, who were vastly varying in age, in
demographics, and in our stories that had brought us together.
He spoke about his personal experience at Onsite and said that
as radical and life-changing as the week ahead would be for us,
the most significant part of the journey would be going home and
waking up each day to make a two-degree shift.

The two-degree shift he spoke of, though small, is what takes
the current trajectory of our lives and shifts it ever so subtly, in the
dailiness of our decisions, reactions, and responses, and radically

changes the place we end up. Even just two degrees is life altering. Years later, I remain cognizant of the two-degree shifts I can make in my everyday life and how those small shifts can drastically change the direction I am heading and, ultimately, my destination.

Being pregnant for the first time with a sweet baby boy was a season I had dreamed about my whole life. Given my prior history of an eating disorder, with a relapse and years of recovery, I'd always anticipated this season with caution and intentionality, ensuring that I was doing the personal and spiritual work to create healthy mindsets, behaviors, and habits that would guard and protect me as I entered a phase of tremendous change in my body.

After years of verbally berating myself and physically pushing my body beyond its limits, while concurrently starving it of the nutrition it needed, I've spent the last ten years learning to be kind to it, to nurture it, respect it, and love it. While pregnant, I saw my body's shape and composition change weekly, and I leaned into the change and embraced it rather than resisting it and slipping into that familiar cycle of control.

With my changing shape, workouts were starting to get tougher, and I noticed that even movements I used to do every day, like push-ups and squats, were becoming more challenging. I had to modify certain movements to accommodate my new shape and load.

When I walked into the clinic for my twenty-four-week appointment, I knew I had gained weight, but that was expected. I stepped up on the scale and a wave of panic hit as I watched a number register that I had never before seen. Completely distracted for the rest of the appointment, all I could think about was the number I had seen on the scale. But as I pushed the elevator button for the first floor and walked out into the chilly air that

December morning, I physically held my hands open, symbolic of relinquishing the control that I have always craved and grasped for, especially in my unhealthier moments as a type Eight.

That was the work I'd spent the last ten years doing: opening my hands to relinquish control. That afternoon I still caught myself flashing back to that moment on the scale, feeling the familiar wave of panic and reflexively wanting to *do* something about the number I had seen, but beyond that, the weight slowly faded into its rightful place in the back of my mind. In the coming days and weeks, I didn't give it a second thought; my weight didn't have power over me, and it didn't rule my mind or control my behaviors.

I didn't wake up one day having arrived at the place where I was able to let that number be just that, a number, and get on with my life. It came over the span of months and years, waking up each morning and making that two-degree shift with my mindset, behaviors, and actions. It came by the refining work of the Holy Spirit, the work that only he can carry out, the work that he does best in the quiet, still moments of our souls, when they are open and willing to be molded and shaped into the likeness of God, to exhibit the virtue and the essence we have uniquely been given.

That two-degree shift is very much at the heart of our spiritual journey of transformation with the Enneagram. It may not feel like the mindsets, habits, and changes we are making daily are doing much, but those two degrees, that small shift, tremendously impacts your spiritual growth trajectory. That's one of the hard parts of the spiritual journey—so often the fruit of your labor takes years to see its yields. But when you do see the results of the work that has been done, when you are able to taste the goodness of the Lord in your life, the reward is so sweet and satisfying.

(14)

RETURNING HOME

SITTING DOWN TO WRITE THESE FINAL
chapters, I want so badly to offer you some tied-up, put-together,
step-by-step solution to your spiritual stagnation, a formula to
quell the disconnect you have felt from God or may currently be
feeling. But, as a type Eight through and through, I just can't offer
you something that isn't the truth, that isn't reality.

The reality is that we live in this in-between place, alienated
by our sin and in pain because of our suffering, both of which are
often highlighted through the lens of the Enneagram. The tension of the two is where we live each day, fumbling and faltering
along in this journey of faith.

But not once has God left us—neither in our sin nor in our
suffering has he forsaken us. We may have wandered through
seemingly endless wilderness seasons, be it through our own sin
or tough life circumstances, or a mix of both. But in those wilderness days, as he was with the Israelites, God was always with us.

Our sin certainly has the ability to estrange us—the greed

and gluttony, pride and envy, the resentment that can overtake us with a malignancy. We are like the sons in the parable of the prodigal son. Maybe we were the younger son, squandering what we were given in reckless and wild ways, living selfishly, straying to a distant country far away from home. Or perhaps we've been the older son, dutifully carrying out the responsibilities of a "good Christian" in years of faithful service, only to find a bitterness, anger, and resentment that results in a hardness of heart and a hatred we've harbored toward our brother and father. Maybe we still show up on Sundays, but we are spiritually as far off as our prodigal brother—stagnant, estranged, disconnected, and detached. Regardless of which brother we resonate with, sin has the same outcome: separation.

And yet we are also sufferers. Sinners, yes, but sufferers too. We are heavy-laden by shame, trapped by fear, compelled by our anger for all that is wrong and unjust in the world. The core emotions and Enneagram triad we are situated in speaks to the suffering we feel on a deep level. For each Enneagram type, perhaps shame, fear, and anger are what most remind us of our humanity. Like the thorn in Paul's flesh (2 Corinthians 12:7), they're a constant reminder that we live in between the finished work of the cross and the "not yet" of the second coming of Christ. And this is the suffering we endure.

The multifaceted framework of the Enneagram can help us examine parts of both our sin and our suffering, but when distilled down, spiritually speaking, the call is the same for each type: *come*. Perhaps our standoffishness, our spiritual stagnation, was partly because we never really understood the heart of God. Maybe similar to the younger son, the prodigal, we never really knew the kind heart of our Father. We expected a judgmental, angry God, one who was as ashamed of us as we were of ourselves. One who would be standoffish toward us after our days of wandering and squandering. But instead, we're met with the most lavish outpouring of love. A robe to replace the fig leaves we'd sewn together to cover our shame. A signet ring solidifying our identity. A place at the table.

Maybe similar to the older son, we forgot the good heart of our father. We had grown cold and aloof, thinking that his heart toward us must mirror ours toward him. We remained in faithful service week after week, year after year. We *knew* that he was good and gracious, kind and gentle, loving and forgiving. But we forgot.

On our journey home, we are forced to confront the most painful parts of ourselves, the sin that entangles us, the suffering we endure, our greatest failures. As agonizing as it may be to go back to the place of failure, where we turned away from God in our prodigal living or aloofness and spiritual apathy, we find that it's in this very place that he meets us with his deepest mercy.

Weary from the weight of our sin and crushed beneath circumstances of suffering, we are invited into the rest that comes through communing with Christ. That is the call home, which is about *coming*. Coming back, whether from a physically distant land like the prodigal son or from a spiritually far-off place like the older son, to find rest from our toiling and striving, from our labor and the heavy loads we carry.

In our homecoming, we find that in our wandering and wondering, our aloofness and apathy, he has never let us go. And maybe even in our wanderings he was still leading us by way of the wilderness, patiently and gently, not wanting us to perish— not pushing, prodding, or imposing anything on us, but with the open invitation to come. To come and find redemption for our sins, reprieve from our suffering, and rest for our souls.

When you've wandered or grown cold toward God, let the spiritual practices for your type and triad be a guide. Allow silence (types Five, Six, and Seven) to renew your mind. Let stillness (types Eight, Nine, and One) recenter your gaze on him and realign your desires with his. Find solitude (types Two, Three, and Four) that reconnects your heart to your Creator.

- **ONES**, know that no amount of striving will secure you a seat at the table. The prerequisite for connection isn't perfection—it's that you simply come.
- **TWOS**, return home and receive love without the requirement of serving and caring for others. Come—you are deeply and dearly wanted here.
- **THREES**, your belovedness can be neither measured nor merited. Because you are a son or daughter, your homecoming is your Father's greatest delight.
- Know, dear **FOURS**, that the story didn't end with wilderness wandering, darkness, and death. The pain and separation can't compare to the joy that awaits your homecoming.
- Type **FIVES**, come, but don't bring anything—it's already taken care of. What you need awaits you at home.
- Weary **SIXES**, cease striving. Come in courage. Fear does not define your past nor will it direct your future.
- Type **SEVENS**, the death, separation, and loss from the crucifixion wasn't final. Yet that magnitude of pain brought everlasting life and abundant joy. Enter into the joy that awaits you.

- Oh, dear **EIGHTS**, that you would know that betrayal isn't the final blow. Mercy will always meet you. Come home and be held.
- And finally, to the **NINES**, come home to be comforted amid the troubles and trials of this world. Perfect peace is coming, but in the meantime, rest here awhile.

To the weary wanderers, spiritual vagabonds, and those with threadbare faith—the invitation stands: *come home.* There are no prerequisites, requirements, or fine print to read. Your burden wasn't meant to be borne alone. Your weariness is welcome. Jesus is waiting to give you rest from your striving and suffering. Come home.

CONCLUSION

The Journey Onward

TO SEE OURSELVES AND OTHERS AS GOD SEES us—as beautifully and wonderfully made, and with empathy—is the thread that connects us together and one of the unique gifts of the Enneagram. As the church, collectively speaking, we love to capitalize on how we have been created in the image of God, uniquely.

But we quickly become divisive when the diversity doesn't fit our ideal. When my type Three husband and I go head-to-head over matters, our dear friends Cole and Ashley remind us to examine closely what is a moral versus amoral issue. Sitting here now, I can't name one moral issue Justin and I vehemently disagree on. But in the amoral camp, we could fight to the death.

Many times, empathy is where peace begins. "If it is possible, as far as it depends on you, live at peace with everyone," Paul instructed us in Romans 12:18 (NIV). I have experienced anger so guttural toward my husband that I've felt like it was impossible to live at peace with him. But when I can look at him with empathy, in his sin and suffering, the deceit and shame that plague him as a type Three, I am more apt to live peaceably with him because I am no different in my own struggles with lust and anger as a type Eight. Empathy isn't giving him a free pass to sin, but it allows me to see the suffering he experiences.

Seeking peace with others, regardless of how divergent our types, beliefs, ideas, or opinions, begins with the pursuit of empathy. Empathy is what allows us to humanize another's sin and suffering. We may not be tormented by shame, entrapped by fear, or gripped by anger, but we have all felt and experienced those emotions. We may not have a proclivity toward avarice, lust, gluttony, or sloth, but we have all waded into that territory in our hearts, minds, and actions.

When our default is compassion and our highest pursuit is love, we can see ourselves and others through the lens of empathy. And here we find that the playing field is even; we are all alike as sinners and sufferers. Stumbling to the foot of the cross, we find level ground, where the Ones and Twos no longer feel the need to perpetually earn their place, where Sixes can come without fear and striving. The grace is for everyone, covering the deception of Threes, the gluttony of Sevens, and the lust of Eights. The Fives' avarice is redeemed, replaced with openhanded offerings, and Nines no longer sink into slothfulness but instead arise and take appropriate action.

The work of redemption will look different in each type's narrative, and the unmerited grace will take on a unique expression, but the call home to Christ, to the cross where that redemption and grace is found, is the same for all. Come, all who are weary and heavy-laden. Come with your sin, come amid your suffering. Be healed and made whole. The redemptive work of Jesus on the cross, the atoning sacrifice and his blood that was shed for the forgiveness of our sins so that we could be made new, is the underpinning of each of our stories and what binds the collective types together in beautiful harmony.

If I don't land this plane soon and with a somewhat succinct conclusion, type Ones will email me after finishing the book, offering an option for an alternative ending. The type Eights probably quit reading after their chapter, and all the Threes are skimming now, looking for bullet points. The type Fours are probably still here, reveling in all the pain, confusion, and incompleteness, so thanks for that.

Writing these concluding words, I have been so convicted of the fact that many times I look down at my life and the circumstances instead of looking up and fixing my eyes on Jesus. I look at this messy first draft and forget that I have an amazing team who will shape this manuscript into something beautiful. I look down at the unsettled circumstances in my personal life right now, my shortcomings and failures. I look at the way others have disappointed and failed me, the surrounding sin and suffering. And when I remember, my response to the invitation is to come, to keep fixing my eyes on Jesus, because he is the source of transformation. It comes from the work of the Holy Spirit in our hearts, not from us. It's the refining flame of the fire that reshapes us. It's not our merit, our strength, our bootstrapping ways of trying to wrangle our lives into niceness and neatness.

The same words I used in the introduction of this book seem fitting to end it with. On your Enneagram journey, *don't be too self-aware or you'll lose sight of Jesus.* Grow and learn, examine your sin tendencies, explore the emotions of your triad, grow in your Enneagram type's virtue. But keep fixing your eyes on Jesus. What we look to, we become like. It may be cliché, but it's true. Keep your eyes fixed on Jesus, where true transformation happens. Look to Jesus, come home to him.

APPENDIX

Continuing the Journey

IF YOU ARE THE TYPE WHO CHECKED THE table of contents and skipped ahead in the book to the chapter about your specific type, and you're skipping ahead in this section, that's 100 percent okay. Skip ahead, read about your type—but then go back. The Enneagram is full of nuance and individuality with each type. Because it is so dynamic—from your wing to the types you gravitate toward in stress and security—there is much to be gleaned from other types besides your core type.

By this point, I hope you have been able to ruminate on the content found in the chapter about your specific type concerning your sin proclivity, virtue, and essence. This appendix will help delineate how to integrate what you discovered, providing momentum for new habits, perspectives, and practices and strategies to get back on track when you fall off.

As you read, pay attention to the types in your triad, the types that wing either side of your type, and the types you go to in both stress and security. They will unearth new ways for you to continue your personal and spiritual growth.

Type Eight

Continue the momentum by

- Surrounding yourself with a few specific people you intentionally practice vulnerability with. Like starting a new workout routine, you may be sore at first, but put in the reps, create the muscle memory, and it will get easier.
- Intentionally putting yourself in situations where you are not the leader or the one in charge. Practice restraint when you disagree with the way someone else is leading, realizing that not everything is black and white. Gray hues are beautiful, even though they are different from what you would instinctively choose.
- Learning to embrace your inner child. I know it may sound stupid and you have more important things to accomplish, but have fun, be silly, and open your heart up. That little kid that still lives inside of you is where the beauty of innocence shines the brightest. The New Testament is riddled with references to the blessed place children have in the kingdom of God (Matthew 18:1–5; Mark 10:15; Luke 18:16).

Get back on track through

- Engaging in the spiritual practice of stillness. As softer, more tender emotions emerge, allow them to do so without stifling them or shoving them away. It will feel painful and pointless but it won't kill you, I promise.
- Being quick to apologize. The type Eight personality is big and boisterous, often unintentionally taking up space from others that is not theirs to occupy. Be ready to say you're sorry when people confront you with feeling "run over" by

your comments or actions, however unintentional it may have been.

- Thinking and feeling. Being a doing-centered type in the gut triad, thinking and feelings are an afterthought or repressed in type Eights. Stop and think before you act or speak or, even more challenging, *feel* about it before you do anything.

See the payoff when

- You are no longer perpetually ensuring that others are not controlling you, and you're no longer under the compulsion to control situations. Your posture becomes one of open hands instead of white knuckles, and while this feels scary, it's ultimately freeing and refreshing.
- You have courageously taken the risk of loving and being vulnerable. Not everyone is out to get you. Betrayal happens but far more often, you'll find that the open arms of another are a soft place to land.
- Not everything is a fight, and you choose to surrender. Even with an overabundance of energy, the constant challenging and endless struggle becomes an exhausting way of life, and it doesn't have to be that way. Surrender doesn't mean losing. Surrender is a strength, for when you are weak, then you are strong (2 Corinthians 12:10).

Type Nine

Continue the momentum by

- Consciously choosing not to merge with others in the small things. If your spouse asks you where you want to go to dinner, and 5 percent of you wants street tacos and queso while 95 percent of you truly does not care, say what you want still! Speaking up, even about the small things, will develop the skill of not merging when it comes to bigger things, like in times of conflict when it would normally be reflexive for you to merge.

- Regularly and actively engaging your mind. While vegging out, scrolling Instagram for a bit, or watching another episode of a show may feel like a form of self-care, be careful that this doesn't put you to sleep relationally and spiritually. Actively engage your beautiful mind in conversations with others that require thoughtfulness and intentionality. Go on a walk or soak in the tub while you meditate on a Scripture verse. The world needs type Nines who are awake and alive, alert with engaged minds.

- Using the phrase "I'm angry." Whoa, I know—that's always been a big-time no-no. But your anger is real and it's there. Practice using this phrase with people who are safe: your spouse, your closest friends, or even in a room all by yourself.

Get back on track through

- Tuning in. You instinctively do this for others, but don't fall asleep to your own feelings, wants, and needs. Learning to tune in will take some time and practice, but it's important work. What do *you* feel? What do *you* want? What do *you* need?

- Owning your space. It's easy to forfeit your space to your spouse, boss, or high-energy friends (hello, type Threes, Sevens, and Eights) but it's yours, and rightfully so. Don't be so quick to give it up, and if you do, take it back. Circle back to the conversation and let the other person know that their response made you feel dismissed. Try using a phrase like the following: "Initially I said I didn't care, but actually, I would like XYZ." Own your space—it belongs to you.

- Creating a short and simple daily checklist and sticking to it. If you've fallen off and realize that slothfulness is starting to emerge, make a daily checklist with a few simple items that get you back on track and moving forward. Combating the tendency to sloth in this way will instill diligence.

See the payoff when

- Conflict, though it likely will never feel comfortable, is no longer something you avoid like the plague. Instead, you are able to consciously engage it when necessary. Passive-aggressive behaviors will fall by the wayside, and deeply buried resentment will begin to dissolve when you acknowledge your anger and appropriately engage it.
- You are awake and alive to the life before you, not falling asleep at the wheel or choosing the path of least resistance. Apathy snuffs out the brilliant light of love and peace that type Nines bring to the world. Wake up, lean in—this is your life.
- Your desires and needs aren't buried deep or a mystery but are known to others and even to yourself. Your presence matters tremendously. The people in your life—those who love you the most—want nothing more than to know how they can love you best by meeting your desires and needs.

Type One

Continue the momentum by

- Actively engaging in an activity you're not stellar at. You don't have to totally suck at it, but don't knock something just because you're not going to do it perfectly. Play volleyball for a rec league, pick up a guitar and strum a few chords, bake a cake, go to a yoga class. This practice will force you to turn down the volume of your inner critic, relax, and maybe even have some fun.
- Letting things be. Leave the laundry overnight and toss it in the dryer in the morning, send that text with a nasty run-on sentence, don't tidy up before your best friend stops by. Practice letting the little things be imperfect.
- Being spontaneous. Go on a last-minute weekend road trip, forget about meal planning and grab takeout, intentionally do something that wasn't part of the plan. Though it may initially spark fear of losing control or the belief that all hell will break loose, it will bring a newfound freedom, carefreeness, and perspective to life.

Get back on track through

- Practicing stillness. You will feel a compulsion to constantly be *fixing* the world around you, but if you can stop and be still, you'll find that even in the midst of imperfection, you can find acceptance. Let acceptance bring a strange sort of peace to your soul.
- Having compassion for yourself. Compassion may feel foreign because in a perfect world, there would be no need for it. But the imperfection of this world and humanity

demands compassion. Start with yourself, which is perhaps the hardest of all. Let yourself off the hook when you make a mistake. Tell your jabbering inner critic that they are not helpful at this moment.

- Reminding yourself that your worthiness is not contingent on your perfection. The Christian cliché is accurate: your beauty shines the most through your brokenness and in your imperfections. I know that sounds absurd, but it's true. Remind yourself of that every day.

See the payoff when

- The black-and-white world around you fades into beautiful hues of gray. There's not always one right way, and when you begin to embrace and believe that, you find freedom and beauty in the world around you.
- You wholeheartedly embrace the truth of Ecclesiastes 3:11 that "He has made everything beautiful in its time." Yes, this means even in the in-between, the not-quite-yet, imperfect world we live in. It is beautiful and it is well.
- Your low-grade resentment and underlying anger begin to dissolve into self-acceptance and self-love. Your integrity is not compromised because of your mistakes but is instead more respected and highly esteemed because of your willingness to embrace yourself and the world around you as is.

Type Two

Continue the momentum by

- Scheduling self-care time. Make an appointment on your calendar with yourself and block it off. Nothing takes precedence over it. You'll be tempted to cancel when a seemingly emergent situation arises with someone you care about—but don't do it. This is time for you to focus on yourself and not on others. It's not selfish; it's necessary for growth.

- Directly expressing your needs to others. This may sound horrifying and unimaginable, but practice expressing your needs to people in the safety of your inner circle. Having needs doesn't mean you are unworthy. As you grow in expressing your needs, you won't experience the rejection you fear. Instead, you'll find that you are *wanted*: wholly and deeply wanted.

- Engaging in the spiritual practice of solitude. Regularly creating a space of solitude with yourself and God will begin to dissolve the feeling of dependence on others for their acceptance and approval.

Get back on track through

- Stopping to think. You are naturally good at doing for others. When you find yourself in a place of feeling unappreciated or undervalued, instead of doing more for others to repress those feelings, stop and think. Ask yourself the question, *What is mine to do?*

- Saying no. If you've slipped into the spiral of saying yes to everyone and everything, get out right now by saying no. If you can't bring yourself to say no, instead say, "Let me check my schedule and I'll get back to you tomorrow." Give yourself time to think it over before you commit. Remember: your value is not found in what you *do* but who you *are*.

- Asking yourself, *What is my motive for helping this person?*

This question will help you reset and realign when you get off track, bringing awareness to any self-serving motives so they can be replaced with true generosity and love.

See the payoff when

- You have appropriately set boundaries and experience the freedom they bring. Setting boundaries can be challenging, but by saying a thoughtful yes and being intentional about saying no, feelings of being unappreciated, leading to resentment, will be replaced with the true joy of giving.
- The playing field in your relationships is no longer uneven and you've released others from their IOU debts. Although these feel like safety nets for when you might need something, they are, in fact, barriers to experiencing the love and care you desire and deserve from others.
- Manipulation, whether conscious or subconscious, is replaced by trust in your relationships. Your own needs are valid and important. Entrusting them to others negates the need for manipulation in relationships.

Type Three

Continue the momentum by

- Asking yourself, *Is this the truth, really?* before you begin to tell a story. Bringing subconscious deceit into consciousness is something that takes practice. Asking that question will propel you on your journey toward authenticity.
- Scheduling time on your calendar for "personal work" and honoring it the same as you would with any professional

commitment. Feelings can be time-consuming and tedious to tend to, but they are markers of what is going on in the interior chambers of your soul and cannot be neglected. Schedule time to meditate and journal or to simply stop and breathe.

- Placing an index card on your mirror that says "You are loved simply for who you are." Read it every morning and night when you brush your teeth, while you stare at your reflection. Begin to see *who* is behind those masks and roles. It's not an empty shell like you may fear.

Get back on track through

- Calling up a close, trusted friend and telling them the truth. If you've been deceiving yourself or others, own it. If you've gotten caught up in your success and image, prioritizing that over your spiritual growth, talk about it. Telling the truth is where liberation begins, and you might be surprised to find that when you tell the truth, you're more deeply loved than you would have dared believe.

- Stopping to ask yourself, *What am I feeling right now?* Slowing down and tending to your feelings is what diverts you from careening further off track toward catastrophe. Shame, fear, and anger are powerful motivators—especially shame. Tend to these feelings. Don't box them up and put them on the shelf to deal with "later," because "later" will never be convenient and thus will never come.

- Starting sentences with the phrase, "If I'm being honest . . ." Sometimes, saying a phrase out loud will trigger a much-needed reset in our minds and hearts. This phrase can help you recognize when you may be placing too much worth in the value you provide rather than in *who* you are.

See the payoff when

- You can just be. You will find those people, though likely only a few, who you can simply *be* with. The masks you've worn and the roles you've played fall away because you know you are loved, wholly and truly, for *who* you are. Those people are a healing balm for your soul.

- You can engage in an activity without it sparking competition or comparison. It sounds impossible, intriguing, and altogether intoxicating, but it's doable. Play a game, do something creative, go on a hike—engage in an activity for the pure love and enjoyment of it.

- Your work is not your identity but rather a way to gift your strengths and skills to the world. The truth that your work is something you *do* and is not attached to *who* you are may initially be terrifying but can become liberating.

Type Four

Continue the momentum by

- Inviting your emotions to take the passenger's seat. Give them names if that helps. You can offer Sally Shame, Fred Fear, and Adam Anger a seat in the car—but remember that the driver's seat is for you. Your emotions will always be along for the ride, but they don't need to drive.

- Taking action today. Your creative ideas are too unique and beautiful to never be brought to life. Buy the domain, pull out the canvas and brushes, schedule a meeting with your friend who is great at strategizing and planning, and get going. Taking action physically will also help you take action emotionally and spiritually.

- Recognizing the feeling that something is missing isn't indicative of something missing *in you*. This world is broken, and it's in a holding pattern until Jesus returns. You feel this truth more profoundly than most, but it is not to be confused with something being inherently missing or broken inside you.

Get back on track through

- Bringing yourself back to the present. Envy can take over when you lose yourself in past events or possible future states. Bring yourself to the present through meditation or setting a timer for five minutes and breathing, noticing each inhale and exhale.
- Practicing gratitude for what you have rather than fixating on what's missing. Each night before you fall asleep or each morning when you wake up, jot down five things from your day that you are thankful for. Keep a running gratitude list on your phone, and each time you feel the grip of envy on your heart, pull out the list and note five things you are grateful for, no matter how small.
- Embracing the ordinary moments of today. Rather than reminiscing over yesterday's extraordinary moments or dreaming about tomorrow's, ground yourself in the present, even if it is boring and ordinary (many days in life are).

See the payoff when

- Gratitude is a reflexive response. It takes practice, but with time and effort, you can replace the knee-jerk response of envy with a deep, abiding, grounding gratitude.
- You believe the truth that God sees you through the same lens of beauty and wonder through which you see the

world. You are not fundamentally flawed but complete and chosen.

- Emotional volatility is traded for steadiness. You will never lose your emotions, but you no longer have to be lost to them. You—not your feelings—are in the driver's seat.

Type Five

Continue the momentum by

- Being an active participant. Engage in the group conversation, pull up a chair and play board games at the next family gathering, join a committee and take a role. Joining in activities like these will help you become a participant, relationally and spiritually, rather than a spectator.
- Sharing more of who you are with others. Holing up in your interior castle will sound safer and far more appealing, but practice coming out to open up and share yourself with the ones who love you the most. We were not created to live and exist alone but in fellowship with other believers.
- Practicing generosity. Give away what you have, whether it's money, time, knowledge, or skills. Practice this with the belief that there *is* enough because Christ is enough.

Get back on track through

- Opening your hands. Yes, literally—open your hands, palms up. If you've fallen off track and become stingy (even unintentionally) with your resources, time, or love and affection, this practice will help you release your grasp.
- Allowing others to care for you. Your self-sufficiency

isolates you from others, and ultimately from God. So much of the beauty we experience with fellow believers is when we allow our needs to be met. People are a tangible, human example of the way God cares for us.

- Beginning sentences with "I feel" instead of "I think." It's reflexive to hole up in that inner castle—after all, that's where you do your best thinking. But bring to the surface those feelings that lie underneath, and follow them up with actions to offset all the thinking.

See the payoff when

- A scarcity mindset is no longer your default. Abundance is yours in Christ and overflows into every other area of life. This truth will abide and keep you rooted when scarcity and fear threaten.
- Relationships aren't seen as a threat but as a soft place to land. You may only ever have one or two people you feel like you can truly let your guard down with, and that's okay. Let relationships be a respite and an invitation to emerge from your interior.
- You are neither attached nor detached. With detachment comes disconnection, but nonattachment from resources enables space and capacity to connect with others on an emotional and spiritual plane.

Type Six

Continue the momentum by

- Making a decision and rolling with it. If it's about what to wear, where to eat, or what brand to buy, make a decision and don't think twice about it. This will aid you in turning down the volume of self-doubt and trusting your instincts (even if it's just for shampoo) so you can trust yourself in bigger things.

- Being spontaneous. Don't let a lack of planning and preparation dictate your decision. If something does go awry, you have exactly what it takes to meet whatever situation arises.

- Writing affirmations for yourself on index cards and reading them out loud each day. These could be Scripture passages, something encouraging someone has said, or a belief you are trying to instill—write it down and read it back to yourself. These will be stockpiled in an arsenal for when self-doubt tries to destroy you.

Get back on track through

- The practice of silencing the mind by engaging in prayer. It's much harder than it sounds, but silencing the self-doubt that echoes through your mind is crucial for you. Self-doubt may come along for the ride, but it doesn't get to drive.

- Stopping the endless strategizing. While it feels like strategizing and planning will give you the security you desperately desire, this is actually an obsession that is feeding your fear and anxieties. Stop it in its tracks. Ground yourself in mindfulness and prayer. Then take the next step.

- Incrementally memorizing Matthew 6:25–34. Start with the first word, then the first line. When you get on the hamster wheel of self-doubt and worry, focusing your mind on the task of memorizing Scripture will arrest the spiral, and the truth of that passage will ground and guide you.

See the payoff when

- Fear is a factor, not the decision-maker. Fear may be felt but it doesn't get to dictate the direction you take.
- You've learned to trust yourself. Instincts are not the enemy and courage doesn't come when there is certainty. Once you have first and foremost placed your trust in God, you can begin to trust in the way you are wired and step out in courage.
- Your faith rings louder than your fear. Your fear will never entirely dissipate on this side of heaven, but your faith—the assurance of things hoped for and conviction of things unseen (Hebrews 11:1)—will be the anchor point of your soul.

Type Seven

Continue the momentum by

- Allowing yourself to be bored. I know—it sounds awful, but it won't kill you. Sometimes life is boring, and that's okay. Learn to not maximize events beyond what they are at every lackluster juncture in life.
- Practicing being present. Put your phone down, stop planning the next international getaway in your head, and be present in the moment to the people and space surrounding you. This doesn't mean never daydreaming or planning fun adventures, but practicing being present will help you develop the necessary muscle memory to be present in the more painful moments of life, without escaping.
- Choosing a few friends to intentionally and regularly go deep with. It's easy to bounce from one social circle to the

next, but transformation happens in the context of community, not with acquaintances.

Get back on track through

- Resisting the urge to reframe pain. Your most important seasons of growth in life are often ones that are exceedingly painful. Reframing the pain robs it of its ability to carry out the work of transformation.
- Practicing moderation. Saying no is required sometimes. When you find yourself caught in the frenetic frenzy of life, practicing moderation by saying no to another commitment, another drink, or another night out is grounding and necessary.
- The spiritual practice of solitude. Solitude with yourself and God brings you a sobriety of mind and a grounding wisdom that's much needed after spending so much of your day engaging and interacting with others.

See the payoff when

- Being present to the pain—not medicating, reframing, or downplaying it—allows you to experience the fullness of joy.
- You find that sobriety of mind isn't synonymous with boredom. Being grounded in the present, rather than constantly thinking about and planning the next fun thing, provides a portal for connection to the people surrounding you in the moment.
- Leaning into the pain, you find not only that you will survive it but that you will be held and comforted by God and others through it.

Spiritual transformation doesn't happen overnight. Just like physical and personal growth, it takes time. It's a process. But it's that two-degree shift that you wake up and make each day that dramatically changes the trajectory of your life. In Philippians 1:6, Paul wrote, "And I am sure of this, that he who began a good work in you will bring it to completion at the day of Jesus Christ." The work of transformation will be completed—maybe in two-degree increments at a time, but he will indeed see it through.

RESOURCES

What Is the Best Enneagram Test?

This is the most frequently asked question I get about the Enneagram. This is not a popular answer but it's the truth: I don't recommend taking a test. The reason I don't recommend a test is that due to the subjective nature of any personality assessment tool, tests can be wrong.

The first Enneagram test I took in high school typed me as a One. It made sense on paper and seemed right, but when I started reading about the different types, I found that while my behaviors aligned with the type One, my motivations aligned with the type Eight. That's why I am a huge proponent of reading about your type, listening to podcasts or audiobooks on the Enneagram, and dialoguing about it. After all, the Enneagram originated as an oral tradition, and I believe this is one of the reasons why.

However, I do see value in tests. For instance, if you're brand new to the Enneagram, a test can act as a springboard to send you in a certain direction of discovery. For people who want to take an assessment, I recommend the Wagner Enneagram Personality Style Scales (WEPSS) test. (This is my personal opinion; I'm not affiliated with them in any way.) It's the only Enneagram test that has been researched, standardized, and statistically validated, achieving the standard of professional review in the Buros Center's *Mental Measurements Yearbook*,[1] a recognized appraiser in the field. The WEPSS is the only Enneagram inventory made available online for sale on the Western Psychological Services website, which speaks to its credibility as well.

While the WEPSS assessment will give you a top score in a dominant type, you will also get a percentage breakdown of how you scored for all nine types. This is where I recommend that people take their top three scores and go read about those types. For example, I take this assessment every few years and typically, my top three types are Eight, Three, and One. While many parts of my personality and behaviors overlap with types Three and One, my motivations and core desires align with the type Eight, which is why I identify as that type.

Here's the catch: it's twelve dollars to take the test.

So naturally, the next question I'm asked is, what's the best *free* test to take?

My question back is, when was the last time you spent twelve dollars on your personal growth?

We've all spent twelve dollars on sillier and more frivolous things than an assessment to help us grow and better understand ourselves. And since you know how I feel about tests, here are the books and podcasts that I highly recommend to anyone looking to get more out of the Enneagram.

Personal Growth

The Complete Enneagram: 27 Paths to Greater Self-Knowledge by Beatrice Chestnut
Enneagram Made Easy: Discover the 9 Types of People by Renee Baron and Elizabeth Wagele
The Road Back to You: An Enneagram Journey to Self-Discovery by Ian Morgan Cron and Suzanne Stabile

Relational Growth

Becoming Us: Using the Enneagram to Create a Thriving Gospel-Centered Marriage by Beth and Jeff McCord
The Enneagram in Love and Work: Understanding Your Intimate and Business Relationships by Helen Palmer
Enneagram Life: Personal, Relational, and Biblical Insights for All Seasons by Elisabeth Bennett
The Path Between Us: An Enneagram Journey to Healthy Relationships by Suzanne Stabile

Spiritual Growth

60-Day Enneagram Devotional Series by Elisabeth Bennett
The Gospel for the Enneagram, a forty-day devotional series by Tyler Zach

Podcasts

Enneagram + Marriage with Christa Hardin

The Enneagram Journey with Suzanne Stabile

Typology with Ian Morgan Cron

Your Enneagram Coach: The Podcast with Beth and Jeff
     McCord

ACKNOWLEDGMENTS

MOM AND DAD, YOU WERE MY BIGGEST champions growing up. Maybe you worried some days, but I never knew. You just kept entrusting me to Jesus who is now forever the keeper of my soul. Mom, your patience and kindness in teaching a severely dyslexic little girl to read and write is a large reason why this book exists today. Dad, your continual encouragement and belief in me—that I could do and be anything I wanted to be when I grew up—is why I became a writer. I am forever grateful that you were chosen to be my guides throughout this life. I love you both so much, thank you, thank you.

Justin, my very best friend throughout the years. We've dreamed a lot of dreams together; many have come true. This book was one of them. I could not have imagined what our lives would hold when I said yes to being your girlfriend at sixteen, but I am deeply grateful for what has been and eternally hopeful for what is to come. I'm glad you are the one to walk with me through this life until we are home in heaven at last. I love you.

My sweet baby, Jack. It only seems fitting that everything about your birth and the parallel birth of this book were unexpected and beyond my control; an invitation for me to surrender. Six hours after submitting the proposal for this book, you came crashing into this world, and I have never been the same. You are a sweet, snuggly, silly, and curious little boy, and it is my greatest honor and joy to be your mama. I love you to the moon and back, Jack!

Mandy Johnson, Rachel Miller, Johanna Vann, and Kelsey Chapman, our Tuesday night writing group was an unforeseen yet rich gift the pandemic brought. Thank you for being my creative champions, for sharpening me as a writer, and for your consistent friendship.

Randy and Shelia, Cole and Ashley, Patrick and Molly, Chelese, and our East Side community group: I slipped into the pews as a spiritual vagabond and you all became the living, breathing body of Christ, the church, to this estranged soul. You fought for our family through the fiercest battle, the fight of our lives (I can still hear Ashley's voice saying that phrase). Thank you for loving our family, for bringing us meals, holding Jack, giving me time to write and heal and rest. I am eternally grateful for this community.

Brigitta Nortker, your kindness and friendship has been a rich gift through the editing process. Your fingerprints are all over this manuscript, your brilliance made this book something that I never could have.

Kathryn Notestine, thank you for polishing this manuscript with precision and preparing it to launch into the world. You were so kind and gentle with this "baby," patient with my crazy ideas, and you carried this project to completion. I am so grateful you were part of this team!

Mark Glesne, Erica Smith, and the whole team at Thomas Nelson, thank you for your kindness, encouragement, and belief in me. It has been such an honor to labor, bringing this book into the world, alongside you all. Amanda Bauch, your thoughtful comments and edits inspired deeper thought and inspiration.

Meredith Brock, to have you represent this book as my agent was truly an honor. My trust in you has never wavered. Over the course of my writing journey, I kept a note on my phone with names, agencies, and publishers that would be the dream to work with—none of which I had connections to, nor did I have much of an idea how this whole thing worked. You were on that list of agents. I told my husband, "I don't know how, but I'm going to figure out how to have her represent me." Thanks for taking a chance on me.

Tracie Miles, Lysa TerKeurst, and the Proverbs 31 team behind the COMPEL book line, thank you for believing in this message and taking a chance on me as the first.

Enneagram focus group: Annie, Hanna, Courtney, Leah, Leslie, Cassie, Jordan, Jordyn, Caleb, Kimmy, Suzanne, Karen, Christina, Tami, Stacey, Breehan, Alex, Jess, Mara, Jim, Aubry, Elisa, Sammie, Cam, Faulkner, Joana, Meredyth, Mallory, Ashley, Sarah, Lindsay, Leta, and Jo. Thank you for sharing your time, wisdom, and hearts. You shaped this book and sharpened me along the way.

"Thy mercy, my God, is the theme of my song."[1] Whether writing books, taking care of sick patients, holding my baby, or folding laundry, may your mercy, goodness and faithfulness be the theme of my life song, O Lord.

Now there are also many other things that Jesus did. Were every one of them to be written, I suppose that the world itself could not contain the books that would be written.

JOHN 21:25

NOTES

Chapter 1: Origins of the Enneagram

1. Lynn Quirolo, "Pythagoras, Gurdjieff and the Enneagram," *Enneagram Monthly*, April–May 1996, http://www.enneagram-monthly.com/pythagoras-gurdjieff-and-the-enneagram.html.

2. Jacob Needleman, "G. I. Gurdjieff and His School," Gurdjieff International Review, last updated May 24, 2002, https://www.gurdjieff.org/needleman2.htm.

3. Denis R. Janz, ed., *A Reformation Reader: Primary Texts and Introductions*, 2nd ed. (Minneapolis: Fortress Press, 2008), 271.

4. James Abrahamson, "Special Revelation: 'God Speaking in Many Portions and in Many Ways,'" Apttoteach, accessed April 26, 2022, https://www.apttoteach.org/Theology/Bible/pdf/204_Special_revelation.pdf.

5. Timothy Keller, *Every Good Endeavor: Connecting Your Work to God's Work* (New York: Penguin, 2012), 145.

6. "Pass Notes: Harry Potter," *The Guardian*, October 19, 1999, https://www.theguardian.com/books/1999/oct/19/costabook award.features11.

7. Joe Carter, "The FAQs: What Christians Should Know About the Enneagram," The Gospel Coalition, August 8, 2018, https://www.thegospelcoalition.org/article/the-faqs-what-christians-should-know-about-the-enneagram/.

Chapter 2: The Journey Home

1. The WEPSS (Wagner Enneagram Personality Style Scales) test has been statistically validated, and that's the one I recommend. For more information, see the Resources section.

Chapter 3: Road Map for the Journey

1. Suzanne Stabile, *The Journey Toward Wholeness* (Downers Grove, IL: InterVarsity Press, 2021).
2. Adapted from The Enneagram Institute, "Oscar Ichazo's Enneagram of the Passions" (figure), accessed April 30, 2022, https://www.enneagraminstitute.com/the-traditional-enneagram.
3. *Online Etymology Dictionary*, s.v. "virtue (*n.*)," accessed May 2, 2022, https://www.etymonline.com/word/virtue#etymonline_v_7822.
4. *Merriam-Webster*, s.v. "valor (*adj.*)," accessed April 30, 2022, https://www.merriam-webster.com/dictionary/valor.
5. Adapted from The Enneagram Institute, "Oscar Ichazo's Enneagram of the Holy Ideas" (figure), accessed April 30, 2022, https://www.enneagraminstitute.com/the-traditional-enneagram.
6. Suzanne Stabile "Enneagram Cohort" (workshop, Life in the Trinity Ministry, Dallas, TX, January 2018), https://www.lifeinthetrinityministry.com.
7. Adapted from The Enneagram Institute, "Oscar Ichazo's Enneagram of the Virtues" (figure), accessed April 30, 2022, https://www.enneagraminstitute.com/the-traditional-enneagram.

Chapter 4: Type Eight: Truth and Innocence

1. Brené Brown, *Daring Greatly: How the Courage to Be Vulnerable Transforms the Way We Live, Love, Parent, and Lead* (New York: Penguin, 2012), 38.

Chapter 5: Type Nine: Love and Action

1. George T. Doran, "There's a S.M.A.R.T. Way to Write Management's Goals and Objectives," *Management Review* 70, no. 11 (November 1981), 35–36.

2. Mary Oliver, "Poem 133: The Summer Day," Library of Congress, accessed May 7, 2022, https://www.loc.gov/programs/poetry-and -literature/poet-laureate/poet-laureate-projects/poetry-180 /all-poems/item/poetry-180-133/the-summer-day/.

Chapter 6: Type One: Perfection and Serenity

1. E. B. White, *Charlotte's Web* (New York: HarperTrophy, 1952), 5.
2. Madeline L'Engle, *Walking on Water: Reflections on Faith & Art* (New York: Convergent Books, 2001), 3.

Chapter 8: Type Three: Hope and Authenticity

1. Brené Brown, *Daring Greatly: How the Courage to Be Vulnerable Transforms the Way We Live, Love, Parent, and Lead* (New York: Penguin, 2012), 72.
2. Ian Morgan Cron and Suzanne Stabile, *The Road Back to You: An Enneagram Journey to Self-Discovery* (Downers Grove, IL: IVP Books, 2016), 146.
3. Margery Williams, *The Velveteen Rabbit* (New York: Holt, Rinehart and Winston, 1983), 5.

Chapter 9: Type Four: Origin and Equanimity

1. Frederick Buechner, *Godric: A Novel* (New York: HarperCollins, 1980), 96.

Chapter 10: Type Five: Transparency and Openhandedness

1. John MacArthur, *Luke 11–17*, The MacArthur New Testament Commentary (Chicago: Moody Publishers, 2013), 122.
2. John MacArthur, *Ephesians*, The MacArthur New Testament Commentary (Chicago: Moody Publishers, 1986), 133.
3. Chip Dodd, *The Voice of the Heart: A Call to Full Living*, 2nd ed. (Nashville: Sage Hill, 2015).

Chapter 11: Type Six: Faith and Courage

1. Editorial Staff, "Process Addictions and Abuse," American

Addiction Centers, last updated June 11, 2019, https://americanaddictioncenters.org/process-addictions-abuse.

2. *Farlex Partner Medical Dictionary*, s.v. "organic disease (*n*.)," accessed May 11, 2022, https://medical-dictionary.thefreedictionary.com/Organic+cause.

Chapter 12: Type Seven: Wisdom and Sobriety

1. Thornton Wilder, *Our Town: A Play in Three Acts* (New York: Harper & Row, 1957), 100.
2. Molly Wilcox, "Day 26: When Long-Suffering Is Godly," in Elisabeth Bennett, *The Enthusiast: Growing as an Enneagram 7* (New Kensington, PA: Whitaker House, 2021), 104.
3. Wilcox, "Day 59: The Focused 7," in Bennett, *Enthusiast*, 185.

Resources

1. Jerry Wagner, "About Jerry," Wagner Enneagram Personality Styles Scales, accessed June 7, 2022, https://www.wepss.com/about.asp.

Acknowledgments

1. John Stoker, "The Mercy of God," (1776), Hymnary.org, accessed July 6, 2022, https://hymnary.org/text/thy_mercy_my_god_is_the_theme_of_my_song.

ABOUT THE AUTHOR

MEREDITH BOGGS IS THE WRITER AND HOST of *The Other Half* blog and podcast. She's known for sharing transparently and authentically about the half of life that doesn't make the social media highlight reel, addressing personal and spiritual growth, the Enneagram, and marriage. Her work has been featured in *Lifeway, Relevant, Grit & Virtue, Her View From Home*, Rising Tide Society, YouVersion, and the COMPEL training blog. Meredith is also a critical care transport nurse and a sexual assault forensic nurse examiner who is married to her high school sweetheart, Justin. They live in Nashville, Tennessee, with their sweet and wild boy, Jack.

COMPEL
Writers Training

COMPEL Writers Training is a faith-based online community from Lysa TerKeurst and Proverbs 31 Ministries. COMPEL was designed to help writers find direction for their work, receive practical training, and discover the motivation to keep going.

We've built COMPEL around three pillars:

- Community with other writers and COMPEL leaders.
- Content that is practical and inspiring.
- Connection with experts in the field and unique publishing opportunities.